EYEWITNESS GUIDES

FISH

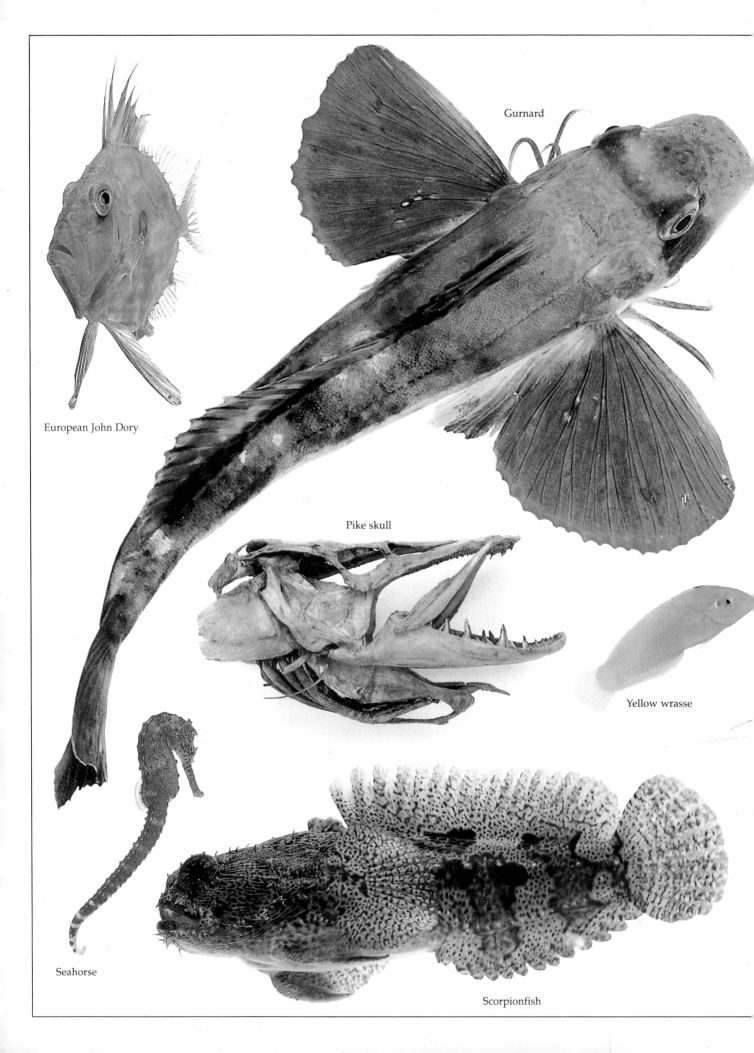

Gurnard

European John Dory

Pike skull

Yellow wrasse

Seahorse

Scorpionfish

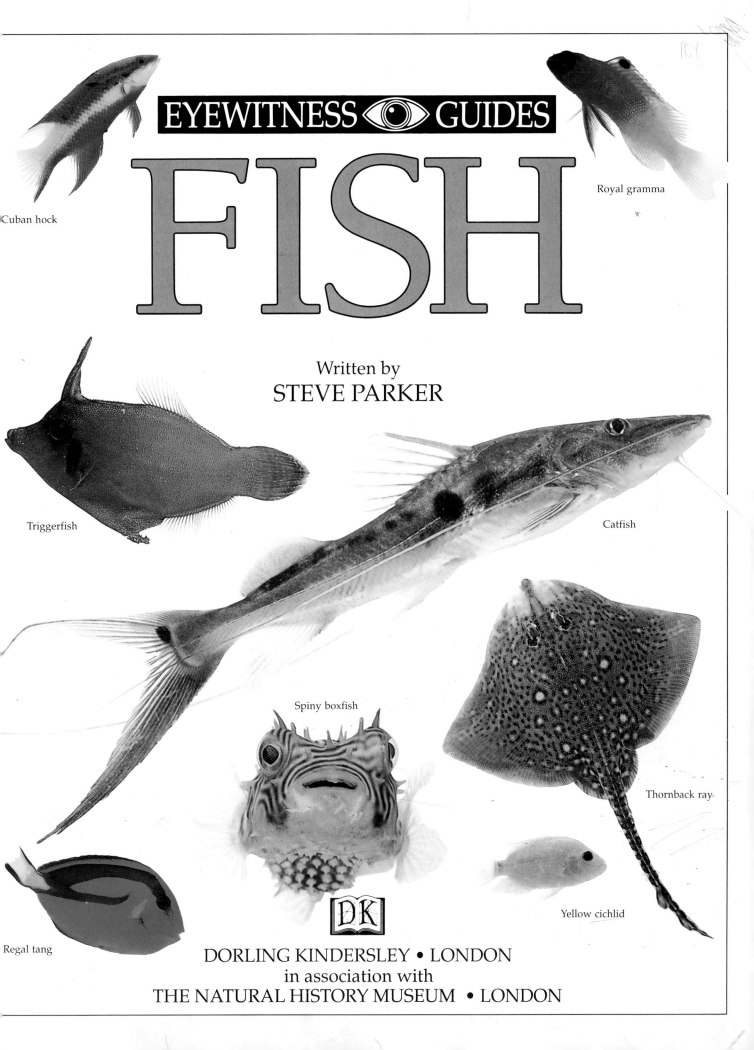

EYEWITNESS ⦿ GUIDES

FISH

Cuban hock

Royal gramma

Triggerfish

Catfish

Written by
STEVE PARKER

Spiny boxfish

Thornback ray

Yellow cichlid

Regal tang

DK

DORLING KINDERSLEY • LONDON
in association with
THE NATURAL HISTORY MUSEUM • LONDON

Twinspot wrasse

Birdnosed wrasse

Project editor Susan McKeever
Art editor Neville Graham
Senior editor Sophie Mitchell
Senior art editor Julia Harris
Editorial director Sue Unstead
Art director Anne-Marie Bulat
Special photography Dave King,
Kim Taylor, Jane Burton and Colin Keates
Editorial consultant Gordon Howes,
The Natural History Museum, London

This Eyewitness Guide has been
conceived by Dorling Kindersley Limited
and Editions Gallimard

First published in Great Britain in 1990
by Dorling Kindersley Limited,
9 Henrietta Street, London WC2E 8PS

Reprinted 1990

Underside of gurnard

Zebra pipefish

British Library Cataloguing in Publication Data
Parker, Steve *1952-*
    Fish
    1. Fish
    I. Title   II.Series
    597

    ISBN 0-86318-411-1

Ribbon eel

Colour reproduction by Colourscan, Singapore
Typeset by Windsorgraphics, Ringwood, Hampshire
Printed in Italy by A. Mondadori Editore, Verona

Contents

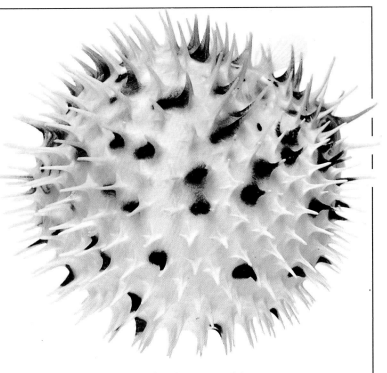

Fully inflated porcupine fish

What is a fish?

THE WORD "FISH" CONJURES UP different images for different people. Some people visualize a streamlined shark, others, a group of brightly coloured tropical fishes darting about a coral reef. Yet others will (wrongly) think of water-dwelling mammals, such as whales and dolphins. Fishes are in fact a vast and varied group of fascinating aquatic creatures, superbly designed for underwater life. There are three main fish groups (p. 9) each of which arrived by different evolutionary pathways, as shown by their body form and internal structure. So different are they, that comparing one with another would be like comparing a mammal with a reptile. However, we can make a few generalizations. Most fishes live in water, breathe by means of gills, possess a scaly body, and swim and manoeuvre themselves using their fins. All fishes are vertebrates, which means that they have a backbone or similar structure, and an internal skeleton rather than an outside "shell". Five main groups make up the vertebrates: fishes, amphibians, reptiles, birds, and mammals. Most of us are aware of the variety of the last four groups. Yet there are about as many kinds, or species, of fishes (some 20,000) as in the other four groups added together!

The mythical mermaid, with a woman's body and a fish's tail, may have been the result of wishful thinking by sailors on long voyages

Fin rays support fin web

Lateral line

Two-lobed caudal fin ("tail", p. 30)

FISHY FEATURES
The common European carp shows most of the typical "fishy features", although at up to 1 m (3 ft) in length it is on the large side. The basic fish shape is tube-like, with a pointed front end, and highly streamlined for slipping smoothly through the water. The carp is "taller" from back to belly than many species, which tells us that it is not a fast swimmer.
There are two main types of fins: paired, (one on each side of the body) and median, or unpaired. The paired fins are the pectorals and pelvics, and they help with steering and manoeuvring. The median fins are the dorsals (some species have up to three), the anal (or ventral), and the caudal fin - usually called the tail. The dorsal and anal fins give the fish stability, like the keel of a sailboat, while in most species the tail provides the power for moving forward.

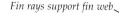

Anal fin

Covering of slimy mucus over body helps fish to slip through water and protects against parasites

Right pelvic fin

Dwarf pygmy goby

BIG FISH, LITTLE FISH
Fishes vary in size more than any other vertebrate group of animals. The world's biggest fish is the whale shark, a harmless oceanic filter-feeder which grows to 15 m (49 ft) long and is over 20 tonnes in weight. The smallest is the Philippino dwarf pygmy goby, at only 8 mm (.3 in) long.

Whale shark

Dwarf pygmy goby (actual size)

What is not a fish?

Various animals are thought of as "fishes" simply because they live in water, but they are not true fishes. Fish-shaped dolphins and seals are mammals, and come to the surface to breathe. Shellfish like mussels and cuttlefish are in fact molluscs. Animals with fishy names include the crayfish and the spiny-skinned starfish, neither of which are fishes.

Atlantic cuttlefish

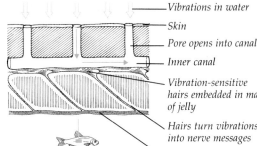

Bottle-nosed dolphin

Dorsal fin (in the carp this is very long and has about 20 fin rays supporting it)

FEELING IN WATER
Water is an excellent carrier of sound vibrations. Fishes can sense these mainly by the lateral line, a fluid-filled tube or canal that runs along each side of the body, under the skin. The vibrations pass into the canal via tiny pores in the skin, and shake tiny lumps of jelly there, which stimulate nerve endings. The fish can "feel" water movements set up by currents and other creatures.

Vibrations in water

Skin

Pore opens into canal

Inner canal

Vibration-sensitive hairs embedded in mass of jelly

Hairs turn vibrations into nerve messages

Sensory nerves to brain

Overlapping scales on body (p. 14)

Eye (many fishes have excellent eyesight)

Nostril

Horny lips

Mouth (for feeding and taking in water to "breathe")

Barbel (fleshy, touch-sensitive whisker)

Operculum (bony covering for gills)

Belly

Scales are almost transparent, letting silvery deeper layers of skin show through and aiding camouflage

Right pectoral fin

FRESH OR SALT?
All water is not the same. Its saltiness has a great effect on a fish's internal chemistry. In rivers and lakes water is absorbed by a fish's body, so the fish must make large quantities of dilute urine. In the sea, the fish's body tends to lose water, so a marine fish drinks a lot and produces only a little, highly concentrated urine. As a result, the vast majority of fishes can only live either in fresh water or in the sea. A few, however, like the salmon, leave the sea to swim up rivers and breed in fresh water. They are known as anadromous species. Eels do the opposite (p. 49) and are called catadromous.

Leaping salmon: making the perilous journey from sea to river

Pisces the fish is a sign of the Zodiac

Inside a fish

THE TYPICAL FISH has many of the body organs found in reptiles, birds, and even mammals like ourselves. A skeleton provides the internal framework (p. 10). The brain receives information about the outside world via sense organs such as the eyes and the lateral line (p. 7) and co-ordinates the complex movements of swimming and manoeuvring which are carried out by teams of muscles. Instead of the lungs of air-breathing animals, fishes possess gills which do the same job – obtaining oxygen. The fish's heart pumps blood around a network of vessels, while its digestive system processes foods into nutrients for growth and repair. Various glands make digestive juices and the body chemicals (hormones) that control development. There are also sexual organs for breeding (p. 40). The scientific study of fish is termed ichthyology.

THE ADAPTABLE SWIM BLADDER
This develops as an outgrowth of the gut (intestine). In many bony fishes it controls buoyancy (top). In some tropical freshwater fishes it connects to the hearing organs and amplifies sounds (middle). In lungfishes it is doubled and absorbs oxygen from swallowed air (bottom).

Swim bladders – front view (left), side view (right)

How fishes breathe

All animals, from eagles to fishes, need oxygen in order to survive. On land, oxygen is contained in the air breathed into the lungs. Water contains oxygen, too, in a dissolved form. Fishes "breathe" in water using their gills. Water flows past the rich blood supply in the gills. Oxygen passes from the water through the thin gill membranes into the fish's blood, and is then distributed around the body.

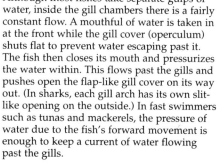

BONY FISH
A typical bony fish like the perch has most of its internal organs packed into the lower front half of the body. The rest of its insides consist of blocks of muscle that produce swimming movements. Some fishes, like the carps, do not have a stomach, but a tightly coiled intestine.

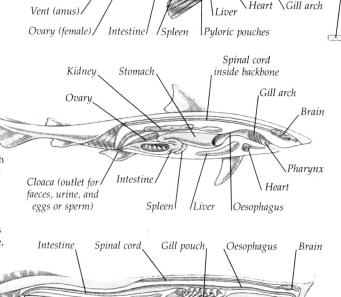

Spinal cord inside backbone — Kidney — Stomach — Swim bladder — Oesophagus — Brain

Urine bladder — Vent (anus) — Ovary (female) — Intestine — Spleen — Liver — Heart — Gill arch — Pyloric pouches

CARTILAGINOUS FISH
A shark has broadly the same internal organs as a bony fish, except that it lacks a swim bladder. Also, near the end of its intestine is a strange corkscrew-shaped structure known as a spiral valve, which probably increases the surface area for absorbing nutrients.

Kidney — Stomach — Spinal cord inside backbone — Gill arch — Brain

Ovary — Cloaca (outlet for faeces, urine, and eggs or sperm) — Intestine — Spleen — Liver — Oesophagus — Heart — Pharynx

JAWLESS FISH
The hagfish's digestive tract is little more than a straight tube, from mouth to anus. Also, it does not "breathe" with proper gills but by gill pouches, which are internal pockets linked to the pharynx and lined with fine blood vessels.

Intestine — Spinal cord — Gill pouch — Oesophagus — Brain

Vent (anus) — Liver — Heart — Single gill outlet — Mouth

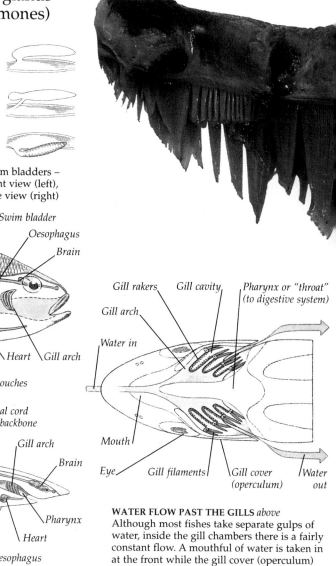

Gill rakers — Gill cavity — Pharynx or "throat" (to digestive system)
Gill arch
Water in
Mouth
Eye — Gill filaments — Gill cover (operculum) — Water out

WATER FLOW PAST THE GILLS *above*
Although most fishes take separate gulps of water, inside the gill chambers there is a fairly constant flow. A mouthful of water is taken in at the front while the gill cover (operculum) shuts flat to prevent water escaping past it. The fish then closes its mouth and pressurizes the water within. This flows past the gills and pushes open the flap-like gill cover on its way out. (In sharks, each gill arch has its own slit-like opening on the outside.) In fast swimmers such as tunas and mackerels, the pressure of water due to the fish's forward movement is enough to keep a current of water flowing past the gills.

THE GILL ARCHES

The gills of a big, active fish such as a tuna must extract plentiful oxygen from the water, to power the great muscular activity. Under each gill cover are four gills, each supported by a curved or V-shaped bony arch. There is a double row of gill filaments on each arch, and each filament is made of many leaf-like folds called lamellae. This gives a large surface area for absorbing oxygen – up to 10 times the area of the fish's body.

Gill filaments (face rearwards), made of leaf-like folds called lamellae

Stiff gill rakers (face forwards) sieve in clean water passing over gills

Bony support of gill arch

Tuna fish gill shown at slightly bigger than life size

BREATHING OUT OF WATER

Some fishes can survive in warm, still, oxygen-poor waters by gulping air and absorbing its oxygen in some way. The 4 m (13 ft) pirarucu (arapaima), a giant of the Amazon region, gulps air into its swim bladder which is linked to the pharynx. The Indian snakehead takes air into the folded, blood-vessel lined pouches of its pharynx.

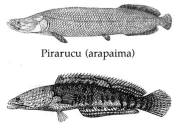

Pirarucu (arapaima)

Indian snakehead

THE MAIN GROUPS OF LIVING FISHES				
Jawless fishes (agnathans)			lamprey, hagfish	About 45 species
Cartilaginous fishes (chondrichthians)			shark, ray, skate	About 600 species
	Sharks and rays (elasmobranchs)			
	Chimaeras (holocephaleans)		rabbitfish, ratfish	20 species
Bony fishes (osteichthians)			coelacanth	1 species
	Lobe-finned fishes (sarcopterygians)	Tassel-finned fishes (crossopterygians)	African lungfish Australian lungfish	7 species
		Lungfishes (dipnoi)		
	Ray-finned fishes (actinopterygians)	Chondrosteans	sturgeon, paddlefish, bichir	36 species
		Holosteans	gar, bowfin	8 species
		Teleosts	perch, carp, and thousands of other "modern" bony fishes	Over 25,000 species altogether

MAIN GROUPS OF FISHES

During the evolution of fishes, thousands of species have become extinct, some leaving fossil remains which give clues as to how present-day groups are related (p. 12). Some quite rare and obscure species are placed in groups all on their own since they are the only living relatives of fishes now extinct. Some, like the lungfish, may represent the ancestors of the first land vertebrates.

The bones of a fish

ALL FISHES HAVE INTERNAL SKELETONS, like us. Sharks and rays have skeletons made from cartilage, instead of bone, and are called cartilaginous fishes. Some fishes, such as the sturgeon, have much of their skeleton made of cartilage. They are called primitive bony fishes. But most fish skeletons are made of bone (bony fishes or teleosts) and have three main regions. One is the skull, which contains the brain and suspends the jaws and gill-arches. A second is the backbone or vertebral column, which bears spines and ribs. The third is the "fin skeleton", the bones and rods which anchor and support the fins and the tail.

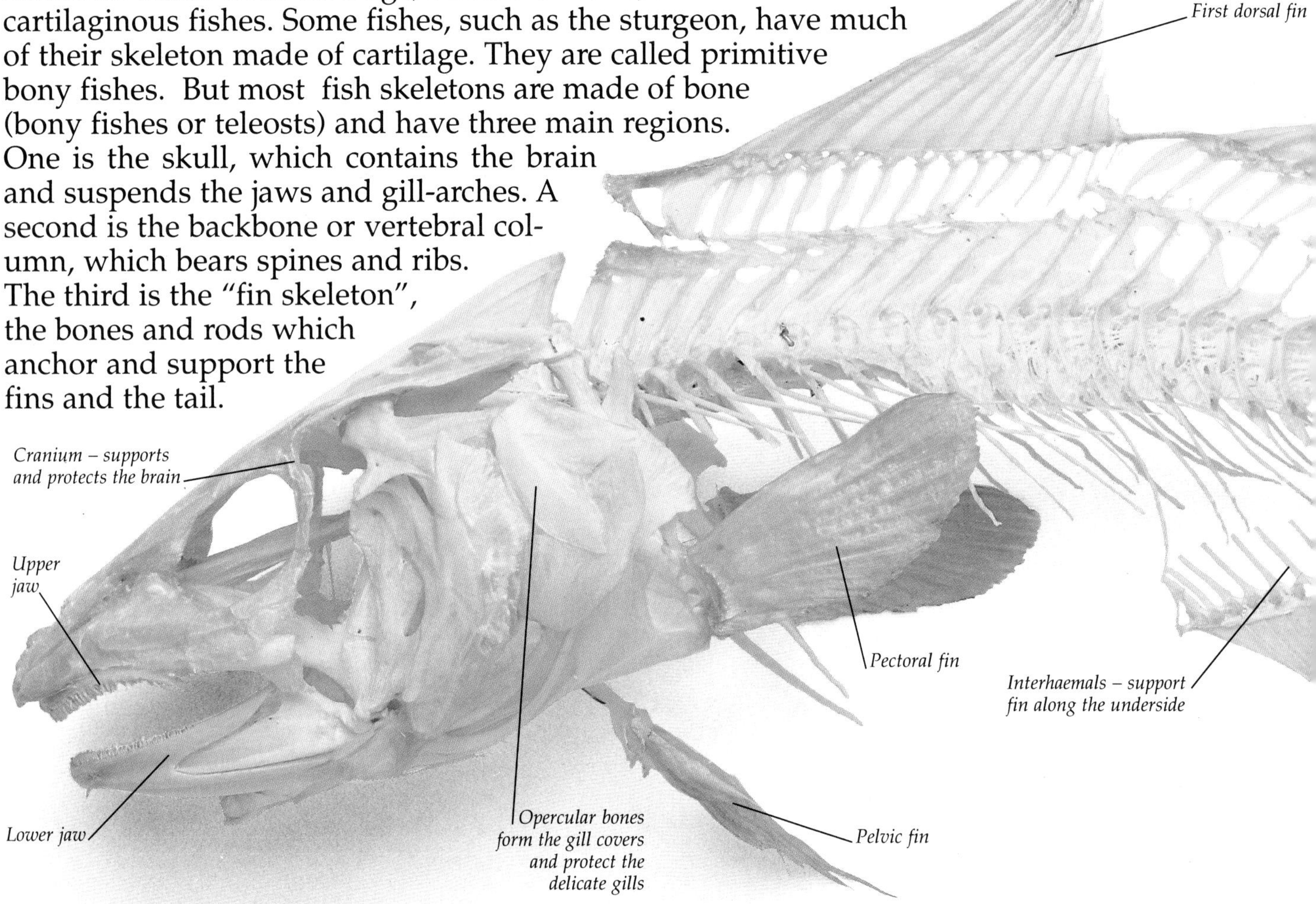

First dorsal fin

Cranium – supports and protects the brain

Upper jaw

Lower jaw

Opercular bones form the gill covers and protect the delicate gills

Pectoral fin

Pelvic fin

Interhaemals – support fin along the underside

A load of old bones

Like most successful groups of animals, fishes have evolved into various shapes and sizes in order to cope with different lifestyles. The shape of the internal skeleton changes accordingly. Portions may increase in size to support and enlarge part of the body, or shrink away to almost nothing when their framework and rigidity are no longer needed. Some unusual parts of skeletons are shown to the right.

Dorsal fin is towards the end of the body

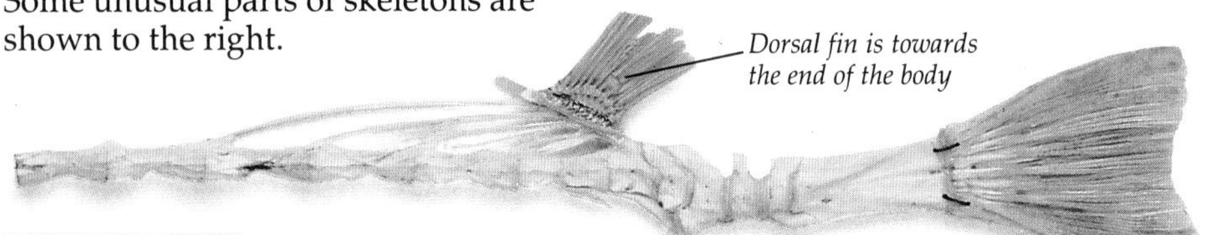

TRUNKFISH TRUNK
The trunkfish's backbone has long supporting rods for its dorsal fin, which is not in the middle of the body but near the tail. This fish's body is covered in a protective box of "chain mail", formed from bony scales. It swims slowly with its fins and tail, since its body is too stiff to flex (bend) in the normal way.

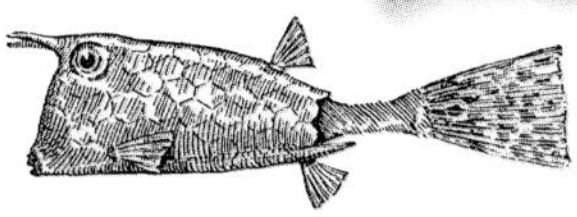

Trunkfish

STOUT, NOT SPEEDY
The backbone of the cascadura, a South American armoured catfish, is stout and inflexible. This fish has rows of overlapping bony plates along its body, sacrificing speed for armoured protection.

BASKER'S BACKBONE
The basking shark is the world's second-largest fish, next to the whale shark. Being a shark, its skeleton is made mainly of cartilage. This is the central portion or centrum of a vertebra, strengthened by a network of mineral-laced fibres.

Centrum is strengthened by a network of fibres

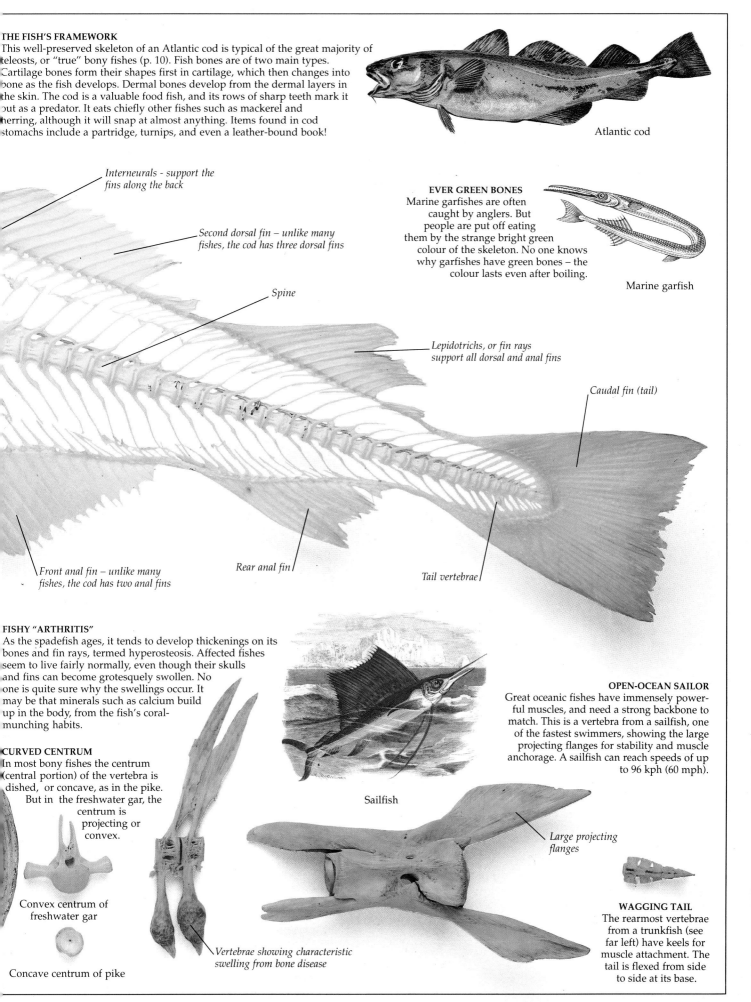

THE FISH'S FRAMEWORK
This well-preserved skeleton of an Atlantic cod is typical of the great majority of teleosts, or "true" bony fishes (p. 10). Fish bones are of two main types. Cartilage bones form their shapes first in cartilage, which then changes into bone as the fish develops. Dermal bones develop from the dermal layers in the skin. The cod is a valuable food fish, and its rows of sharp teeth mark it out as a predator. It eats chiefly other fishes such as mackerel and herring, although it will snap at almost anything. Items found in cod stomachs include a partridge, turnips, and even a leather-bound book!

Atlantic cod

Interneurals - support the fins along the back

Second dorsal fin – unlike many fishes, the cod has three dorsal fins

Spine

EVER GREEN BONES
Marine garfishes are often caught by anglers. But people are put off eating them by the strange bright green colour of the skeleton. No one knows why garfishes have green bones – the colour lasts even after boiling.

Marine garfish

Lepidotrichs, or fin rays support all dorsal and anal fins

Caudal fin (tail)

Front anal fin – unlike many fishes, the cod has two anal fins

Rear anal fin

Tail vertebrae

FISHY "ARTHRITIS"
As the spadefish ages, it tends to develop thickenings on its bones and fin rays, termed hyperosteosis. Affected fishes seem to live fairly normally, even though their skulls and fins can become grotesquely swollen. No one is quite sure why the swellings occur. It may be that minerals such as calcium build up in the body, from the fish's coral-munching habits.

CURVED CENTRUM
In most bony fishes the centrum (central portion) of the vertebra is dished, or concave, as in the pike. But in the freshwater gar, the centrum is projecting or convex.

Convex centrum of freshwater gar

Concave centrum of pike

Sailfish

Vertebrae showing characteristic swelling from bone disease

OPEN-OCEAN SAILOR
Great oceanic fishes have immensely powerful muscles, and need a strong backbone to match. This is a vertebra from a sailfish, one of the fastest swimmers, showing the large projecting flanges for stability and muscle anchorage. A sailfish can reach speeds of up to 96 kph (60 mph).

Large projecting flanges

WAGGING TAIL
The rearmost vertebrae from a trunkfish (see far left) have keels for muscle attachment. The tail is flexed from side to side at its base.

Early fishes

Nearly 500 million years ago, the first fishes swam in the Earth's waters. They had no jaws, fins, or scales like the fishes of today. But early fishes did have a type of backbone – the feature that divides vertebrates such as birds, mammals, reptiles, amphibians, and the fishes themselves, from the rest of the animal kingdom (invertebrates such as insects and worms). The backbone formed a firm yet flexible central brace against which muscles could pull, to propel the creature along. Fishes fossilized well, partly because their skeletons were made of hard bone. Yet another first for fishes was jaws. These were a major advance, since jawless creatures are mostly restricted to sucking or rasping at food. Jaws allowed them to bite and chew on items that were too large to swallow in a single gulp. They were a great success. Today, all fishes except the lampreys and hagfishes have jaws of some kind.

FISHY LANDSCAPE
The first fishes with jaws appeared 435 million years ago, during the Silurian Period. This weird scene shows where they might have swum.

TIME CHART SHOWING EVOLUTION OF THE FISHES

Millions of years ago
500   400   300   Present day

Jawless fishes

Sharks and rays

Fossil bony fishes

Modern bony fishes

Coelacanths

Bony shield protected fish

JAWLESS WONDER
Cephalaspis belonged to a group of extinct fishes called the osteostracans, which were among the first fishes to appear on Earth. This fossil is nearly 400 million years old. Most such early fishes did not possess jaws. They had round, fleshy, sucking-type mouths. The large, bony shield protected the fish's head and gills. These types of fishes were only about 10 cm (4 in) long.

Restoration of *Cephalaspis*

Shark-like fin

TINY SPINY
Ischnacanthus was an acanthodian or "spiny shark". These ancient fishes were somewhat shark-like in shape, and each fin had a strong spine along its front edge. They flourished about 400-350 million years ago and then gradually died out.

FIRST OF THE RAY-FINS
The palaeonisciforms were the first of the bony, "ray-finned" fishes (p. 9) which now make up the vast majority of fish species. At first the rod-like fin rays (lepidotrichs) were parallel to the fish's body, but gradually they splayed out to make a fan shape as in the fins of most modern fish. In this fine fossil of *Palaeoniscus*, from 250 million years ago, the sculpted individual body scales are clearly visible.

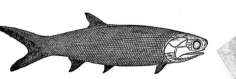

Restoration of *Palaeoniscus*

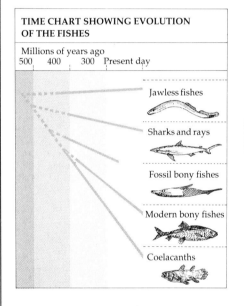

Cartilage struts

Sculpted individual body scales

Scales

ROUNDED HOLOSTEAN
Dapedium dates from the Lower Jurassic period of time, some 190 million years ago. It was a holostean, a member of a group that was common at this time (p. 9). Holosteans had a fully developed back bone, but the rest of the bony skeleton was poorly developed. Today there are still some living species of holosteans, including the gars of North and Central America. The giant gar grows to more than 3m (10 ft) in length and hunts smaller fishes for food.

Large predatory mouth

THE RISE OF THE TELEOSTS
Europholis has the streamlined shape, large mouth, and sharp teeth of a hunter. It is a teleost, or "true" bony fish (p. 9). Teleosts make up the great majority of fish species alive today. These agile and adaptable creatures rose to success some 200-100 million years ago.

This restoration of *Eusthenopteron* shows the bones of the head and internal skeleton

FINS TO LEGS
The slim, predatory *Eusthenopteron* was a primitive lobe-finned fish. Some lobe fins are thought to be related to coelacanths and lungfishes and so are on the ancestral line that gave rise to land-living vertebrates (tetrapods). However, *Eusthenopteron* itself was not a tetrapod ancestor, but merely a "fish" adapted to the conditions of its time.

ALMOST THERE
Teleost fishes such as the small *Stichocentrus* gradually took over the waters from the many fish groups that had gone before (p. 9). With their bony inner skeletons, flexible fins, efficient jaws, and light-weight scales, they had come a long way from the jawless, heavily armoured, tank-like versions such as *Cephalaspis*.

STRUT-FILLED WINGS
Rays have skeletons made of cartilage (p. 9) which is softer and decays more quickly than bone, so it is fossilized less often. Therefore we know less about the evolution of rays and sharks, compared to bony fishes. This specimen, *Heliobatis*, which is a kind of stingray, displays the dozens of cartilage struts in its "wings" (pectoral fins). Rays today are much the same as those that lived millions of years ago.

Flipper-like fins

Famous fish
In 1938 scientists were startled by the discovery in South Africa of a coelacanth. Many fossil coelacanths were known, dating back to nearly 400 million years ago. However, experts had thought they had died out 80 million years ago. But it seemed local people had been catching them for years. They had even been using their scales to roughen bicycle inner tubes before sticking on a puncture patch. More than 100 coelacanths have since been caught, and these fishes have been filmed swimming in the sea near the Comoro Islands, off south-east Africa.

The coelacanth today - still alive and swimming

Scale story

MOST FISHES ARE COVERED in an outer layer of transparent plates called scales. They vary in size and shape, but the average bony fish scale is small and rounded, flexible, and single layered – called a leptoid scale. There are three other basic types of fish scale. Sharks and rays have tooth-like placoid scales, also called dermal denticles. The ancient coelacanth has four-layered cosmoid scales. Ganoid scales, found on gars, are diamond-shaped. Some fishes have no scales at all, but they have extra-tough skin. The "sliminess" of a fish issues not from the scales, but from the skin underneath, which makes a special mucus. This helps the fish to glide easily through the water.

Large reflective scales along lateral line

Ventral fin

Pelvic fin

STURGEON'S SCUTES

Sturgeons, members of a group 135 million years old, have lost most of their scales during evolution. All that remain are five rows of large, flat, scutes that run along the body. A scute from a big sturgeon can be as big as 10 cm (4 in) across.

Sturgeon scute

Sturgeon

NON-SLIP GRIP

For centuries people have appreciated the rough texture of shark skin, using it as a natural sand-paper or non-slip sword grip. Shark and ray scales are different from bony fish scales. They are generally tooth-shaped and called placoid scales or denticles. Each has a bony core fixed in the skin, and a backward-sloping spine. Stroke a shark the wrong way, and you could severely graze your own skin.

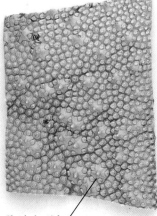

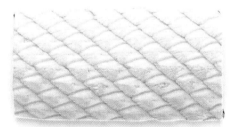

Diamond-shaped interlocking scales

Side view of gar scales showing slight overlap

CHAIN-MAIL SCALES

The North American gar has the closely-fitting, diamond-shaped scales of its many extinct relatives. These ganoid scales link by fibres to form a strong but inflexible suit of chain-mail armour. Tough gar skin covered the ploughs of the early European settlers in North America.

Garfish

COELACANTH SUIT

Unlike the gar, the coelacanth (p. 13) has well-overlapping scales of the four-layered cosmoid type. Each scale is a bony plate bearing small tooth-like spines, a bit like shark denticles.

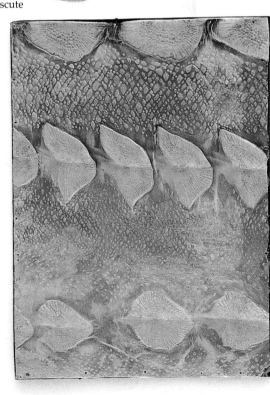

Shark denticle

Sturgeon skin showing three rows of scutes

Mirror carp

SHINING SCALES
With its large reflective scales, the mirror carp is an unusual sight. A type of common carp, the scales appear mainly along its lateral line – leaving the rest of the body "naked". No wonder it is called the mirror carp, as its scales clearly show the silvery reflective skin grains beneath. Another type of common carp, called the leather carp, has no scales at all.

COUNTING SCALES
In most fishes, scales run in a pattern of diagonally-sloping rows, downwards and rearwards over the body. Counting the exact numbers of rows helps to identify a fish accurately. Scales along the body (lateral line) give the number of diagonal rows. Scales from back to belly (transverse line) give the number of horizontal rows.

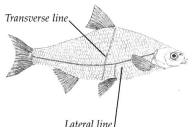

Transverse line

Lateral line

Gill cover

Parts of body without scales

ON A LARGE SCALE
The tarpon's scales are among the largest of the typical leptoid bony fish scales, each being more than 5 cm (2 in) across. They are smooth, with no serrations, and are often used to make decorative jewellery. The tarpon, a power-ful predator, is similar to the earliest true bony fishes.

Tarpon scale

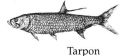

Tarpon

THE RIGHT SCALE
The carp scale is a good example of the leptoid scale found on most bony fishes. Each scale has two plate-like layers – a bony one and a thin fibrous one. Its front end (root) is embedded in a pocket in the lower layer of skin (dermis), while the other end is quite free.

HOW OLD?
Under the microscope, a carp scale shows growth rings, like a tree trunk. Bony fishes have roughly the same number of scales through life; each one grows in time with its wearer. Several widely-spaced rings indicate a season of rapid growth.

COMBED SCALE
Angelfish scales have tiny teeth, like a miniature comb, along the free edge. They are called ctenoid or "comb-like" scales.

Growth rings on magnified carp scale

Spines in skin become erected when porcupine fish is annoyed or scared

THORNY CAT
The thorny catfish has a single row of large, viciously-pointed scutes, like rose thorns, along each side of the body. It also has a strong skull that extends into a bony plate which protects the neck region, while the large fins are edged with toothed spines. Not surprisingly, these South American river-dwellers have earned the nickname of "touch-me-not-fish".

Thorny catfish (a type of armoured catfish)

Row of scutes with sharp thorns

SPINY SCALES
This close-up shows the prickly spines of the porcupine fish. Even laid flat, the kite-shaped bases of the spines fit tightly to give good protection. When the fish is intimidated, it puffs itself up to erect the spines (p. 38).

A riot of colour

MANY FISHES USE COLOUR, not to look pretty, but for serious survival tactics. Fishes have evolved almost every imaginable hue and pattern, for various reasons. Colour is an excellent means of camouflage or defence, or of advertizing a territory. Smooth and silvery greens, blues, and browns camouflage some species in open water; a riot of brilliant reds, yellows, and blues conceal others among the equally splendid colours of a coral reef. Spots, stripes, and patches break up or "disrupt" a fish's normal outline, confusing predators. Other colours might signal that one fish owns this territory, so go away; or another fish is ready to mate, so come here!

Lateral line

Large "pearl" scales

Eye stripe

PEARLY SCALES
In the pearl-scaled butterfly fish, the yellow and orange colours, typical of butterfly fishes, are limited to the tail end. The large pearly scales give a rainbow effect of colour, and the fish's eye is camouflaged by a black stripe

Disruptive vertical stripe on tail

Barbels for finding way and food in muddy water

Clown loach

HIDING IN THE SHADOWS
Loaches swim mostly near the bottom. The clown loach likes to retreat among lake-bottom material, where its broad dark stripes resemble fallen branches or the shadows of plant stems.

Forceps fish

Long, thin forceps-like mouth for nibbling in crevices

False eyespot on dorsal fin may distract predators

False eyespot

TAILS YOU LOSE
The forceps fish has a false eyespot near its tail base. As a predator approaches from behind, intending to attack the "head", the forceps fish swishes its fins and darts off the other way.

Royal gramma

Eye hidden in a stripe

REGAL PURPLE
The startlingly bright "royal purple" front end gave the royal gramma its title. This species is a cave-dweller, so its coloration is unlikely to be used for camouflage. But it is very territorial, and so the bright colours probably make it highly visible as it chases away competitors.

ZEBRA IN THE GRASS
Instead of hiding upright as one long, thin stem of waterweed, like the snake pipefish (p. 23), this zebra pipefish hides horizontally – as about 28 stems!

Dark spot on dorsal fin

Transparent tail makes fish look two-ended

French angelfish

GROWING COLOURS
As this young French angelfish grows, the four vertical bars will deepen to a vivid yellow and the body will darken.

Pale flecks on body will darken to solid olive-green

EYE SURPRISE
Flicking up its dorsal fin, the one-spot yellow wrasse reveals an eye-like dark spot against the brilliant yellow background – a surprise for any predator.

Eye hidden by head stripe

DESIGNER'S NIGHTMARE
A white mustard-lined forehead, zig-zags on the front half of the body, fading into bright yellow at the back, and a false eyespot on the rear of the dorsal fin – it is difficult to imagine a more varied patterning than on the threadfin butterfly fish, from warm Australian seas.

Threadfin
butterfly fish

Gap below eyespot, between rear of dorsal fin and tail fin, resembles a "mouth" facing right

SPOT THE WRASSE
The sea-living wrasses are one of the most colourful of fish groups. This red, white, and green wrasse cruises through seaweed fronds, its spots and splodges drawing attention away from the overall fishy outline.

First spine in dorsal fin can be locked up by second "trigger" spine

Eye is tinted red

DIRTY RED
Scattered darker scales on the Cuban hock's body and the tips of the dorsal and pectoral fins help to give a slightly "dirty" appearance, perhaps aiding camouflage. The eye is tinted red, to match the fish's upper body. This species also has fine decorative fin rays.

Eye concealed by dark facial stripe

Clown
triggerfish

Cuban hock

ALL DRESSED UP
Be a predator. Close your eyes, open them to glimpse at the clown triggerfish for a second, then close them again. With such a dramatic set of contrasting and broken patterns, it is difficult to prepare yourself for an attack on this species.

Tail remains yellow as in young fish

Regal tang

GETTING THE BLUES
The regal tang, a member of the surgeonfish group from warm Atlantic coral reefs, starts out life mostly yellow. Gradually the deep, rich blue extends from the front of the body as the fish matures.

Red flag-like tail may be used to startle predators

Zebra pipefish

Mandarin
fish

SEABED DOODLE
"Scribblefish" is a local name for the mandarin fish, which frequents coral and rocks across the eastern Indian and western Pacific oceans. Like its relative, the dragonet, the male mandarin fish has long spines on the first dorsal fin.

Blue-ringed "eyespot"

Vague dark bands run along back

NOT SO YELLOW
On close examination, the fins and scales of the yellow cichlid show subtle shades of cream, grey, orange, and brown.

Yellow
cichlid

Spine on gill cover, typical of the angelfish group

BLUE BANDED
The striking electric-blue bands of the blue-ringed angelfish are a strong visual signal to nearby members of the same species. However the almost invisible tail disrupts the general fish shape.

17

Continued on next page

Cutting down on colour

Fishes from the world's cooler waters, and those dwelling in the open ocean, have more muted colours and patterns compared to the species of tropical lakes and coral reefs. Many that swim near the surface are "countershaded": darker on the back, and paler on the belly. Light from above brightens the back and shadows the underneath - and so the fish loses its impression of depth and "disappears" into the surrounding water.

Rainbow is the only trout in Europe with a spotted tail

Crescent-shaped pinkish-red rainbow sheen

Small black spots sprinkled over head, body, fins, and tail

Rainbow trout

COLOURS OF THE RAINBOW
A native of California, the rainbow trout has been introduced to many countries for anglers and as a food fish. The name comes from the crescent-shaped pinkish-red band along the side in some individuals.

TENCH IN A TRENCH
Deep olive-green or nearly black, the bottom-living tench becomes just another patch of murky water in the still, muddy, weedy lakes and ponds it frequents.

Very thick base of tail

Tiny scales are almost invisible

Tench

Paler underside for countershading

Large scales have silvery sheen

GLIMPSING A GLINT
The rudd favours lying lazily just under the surface in summer, darting up for drowning insects. Its broad, silvery sheen matches the glinting reflections when seen from above the surface.

Reddish fins

Rudd

GOLDEN BROWN
Exceptionally round-bodied, the muscular crucian carp sports large golden-brown scales to blend in with the dim water of weedy, shaded pools and slow-flowing rivers. It is a close relative of the familiar goldfish

Crucian carp

NO CALL FOR COLOUR
Most fishes that live in dark ocean depths lack colour, but "light up", using luminous organs. This aptly named loosejaw produces a green light.

Distinctive golden scales

Long barbels for feeling the way along the dark bottom

Spot on tail is a "shoaling mark", keeping groups of young together

Freshwater catfish

FLYING THE FLAG
The festa cichlid is one of the many varieties of festive cichlids (also called barred or flag cichlids). Some South American cichlids have been bred to all colours of the rainbow by aquarists.

Fish gets its name from dorsal fin that stands up like a top hat

Hi-hat drumfish

BLACK CAT
So-called because of their whisker-like barbels, catfishes are usually darkly coloured. This freshwater catfish from South America lives mostly on or near the bottom. If it swims to the surface, its underside mimics the dappled effect of light in water.

Vivid stripes

SOUND, THEN SIGHT
Drumfishes or "croakers"are so-called because they make drumming and knocking sounds, especially at breeding time. These noises carry far underwater; as the fishes come nearer, eyesight takes over and they recognize each other by visual signals, such as the vivid stripes on this hi-hat drum.

TOP AND BOTTOM
The blue shark, swimming near the surface is light on the bottom and dark on the top. The carpet shark lies on the bottom and merges well with weeds and rocks.

Blue shark

Panther grouper

Carpet shark (wobbegong)

Large black spots on body

LURKING HUNTER
Named from the spotty big-cat predator, the panther grouper behaves similarly around rocks and reefs. Out of its natural habitat, it is highly visible; but in its speckly natural habitat the pattern of black spots on the whitish body becomes remarkably inconspicuous.

Red eye

Sensory barbels to locate food in mud

Red mullet

GREEN SHEEN
Swimming and feeding near the sea surface, the mackerel uses countershading to advantage. Its back shows a dark metallic greeny-blue sheen, while its underside is pale.

RED WHEN DEAD
By day, the red mullet from European seas shows a reddish-brown back and yellow lower body stripes. But at night it takes on a more marbled appearance. In times past people marvelled at the brilliant shining red that developed when the fish was stressed - that is, being caught and killed.

Yellow stripes along lower flank

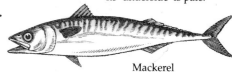

Mackerel

Amazing shapes

Most fishes are the usual "fish" shape, like the cod (p. 10). But there are endless variations on the theme. Long, slim, arrow-like fishes such as the gars are super-streamlined for quick dashes out of hiding. Other species have sacrificed speed for stealth, like the squat, flattened anglerfish which sits on the bottom and awaits its catch. Deep-bodied thin fishes like the angelfishes are flexible and can slip between plant stems and coral formations. Shape, like colour, contributes to camouflage. Waving fins may be disguised as flowing plant leaves, and the entire body might resemble a plant, or even another animal.

DEEP-SEA ROCKET PLANE
Lurking in the depths of the North Atlantic is Harriott's long-nosed ratfish, a holocephalean (p. 9) that grows to 1 m (3 ft) long. With its long, thin snout and tail, and wing-like pectoral fins, it looks a bit like a space rocket plane.

THINLY DISGUISED
Head on, the European John Dory's extremely slim outline (left) is hard to spot as it slowly moves towards its prey. Seen from the side (right), the almost disc-shaped body indicates a stalker rather than a chaser. The John Dory is well protected by the sets of stout spines in front of its dorsal and anal fins.

Rabbitfish

RABBIT'S TEETH, RAT'S TAIL
The rabbitfish derives its name from its rounded snout bearing large cutting teeth, like the "buck" teeth of a rabbit. Its alternative name of chimaera comes from the grotesque monster of Greek mythology.

ELEPHANT'S SNOUT
Elephant-snout fishes, or mormyrids, usually have a down-curved mouth and nose for probing in the mud for food. (The head skeleton is shown on page 34). Peters' elephant-snout fish has a relatively short "snout".

Dorsal fin set well back

Narrow caudal region (peduncle) - useful for fine manoeuvring

Elephant-snout fish

"Trunk" curves downwards

John Dory – side view

Pelvic fins held edge-on to minimize shape

Fins drawn out into fine filaments

Bars on body resemble reed stems

John Dory's minimal outline seen from front

Freshwater angelfish

Eye concealed by dark stripe

Dorsal fin set far back along body

AMAZING GRACE
The angelfish lives in slow-flowing South American rivers. Its crescent shape, body bars and softly waving fins blend perfectly with the current-curved waterweeds. This species is a member of the cichlid group. The similar-shaped but sea-dwelling French angelfish is on page 16.

Long jaws carry sharp teeth

Long-nosed gar

Bars along side conceal fish among weeds and reeds

STRAIGHT AS AN ARROW
Fully streamlined, the long-nosed gar from North American fresh waters can move very fast – but only in short bursts. It ambushes prey by dashing from its weedy hideout. (Its diamond-shaped scales are shown on page 14.)

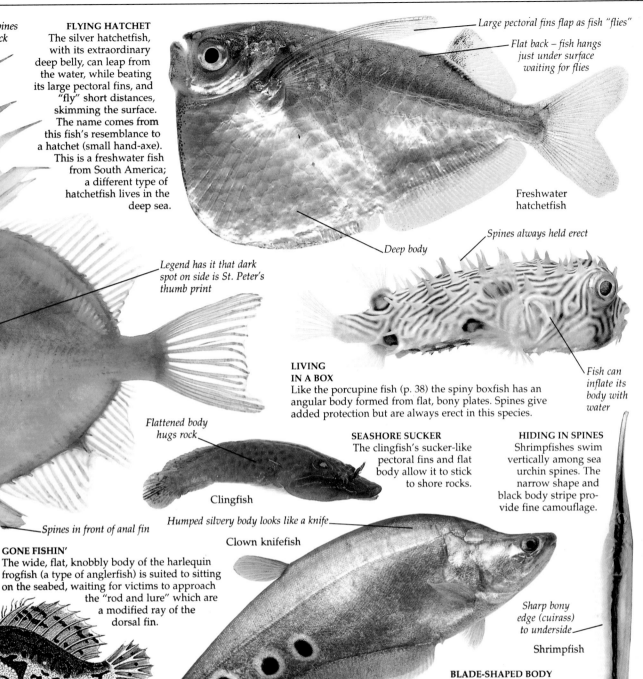

Stout spines on back

FLYING HATCHET
The silver hatchetfish, with its extraordinary deep belly, can leap from the water, while beating its large pectoral fins, and "fly" short distances, skimming the surface. The name comes from this fish's resemblance to a hatchet (small hand-axe). This is a freshwater fish from South America; a different type of hatchetfish lives in the deep sea.

Large pectoral fins flap as fish "flies"

Flat back – fish hangs just under surface waiting for flies

Freshwater hatchetfish

Deep body

Spines always held erect

Legend has it that dark spot on side is St. Peter's thumb print

LIVING IN A BOX
Like the porcupine fish (p. 38) the spiny boxfish has an angular body formed from flat, bony plates. Spines give added protection but are always erect in this species.

Fish can inflate its body with water

Flattened body hugs rock

SEASHORE SUCKER
The clingfish's sucker-like pectoral fins and flat body allow it to stick to shore rocks.

HIDING IN SPINES
Shrimpfishes swim vertically among sea urchin spines. The narrow shape and black body stripe provide fine camouflage.

Clingfish

Humped silvery body looks like a knife

Clown knifefish

Spines in front of anal fin

GONE FISHIN'
The wide, flat, knobbly body of the harlequin frogfish (a type of anglerfish) is suited to sitting on the seabed, waiting for victims to approach the "rod and lure" which are a modified ray of the dorsal fin.

Sharp bony edge (cuirass) to underside

Shrimpfish

BLADE-SHAPED BODY
Knifefishes, such as this clown knifefish, have a long, slim, deep body shaped like a carving or bush knife. The long anal fin joins with the caudal (tail) fin and provides propulsion.

Harlequin frogfish

Knifefish swims by moving long anal fin

Sharp spine under tail

COW-HORNED AND COW-EYED
The cowfish is in the boxfish group (see above). Plates of bone under the skin form a rigid, slab-sided shell with only the mouth, eyes, gills, fins, and ventral opening on its outside.

Cowfish – front view, showing cow-like facial features

Protective front-facing spines like horns of a cow

Flat bony plates on underside

Cowfish – side view

Pipes and horses

THE HEAD OF A CHESS PIECE, the tail of a monkey, a ridged body that seems carved from wood, eyes like a chameleon, and a father who becomes pregnant. This is the seahorse, an unlikely looking fish. In the same family is its cousin, the pipefish. The seahorse swims upright, propelled by a wavering dorsal fin. The small pectoral fins help to steer the animal as it glides along. There are no pelvic or tail fins at all. But there is a tail - tapering and prehensile (grasping), able to grip seaweed stems as the seahorse watches for food. Pipefishes also swim mainly by their dorsal fins and, like seahorses, are well protected by a casing of bony plates. But perhaps the strangest feature of these creatures is that the females lay their eggs "in" the males.

Each male has a fold of skin or pocket-like pouch. Here the eggs develop into fully-formed baby seahorses.

Dorsal fin

Plate-like scales

Head set at right - angles to body

Caribbean seahorse

Prehensile (grasping) tail

Orange sea-whip coral

CORALLED HORSES
Three seahorses decorate a piece of gorgonia coral (orange sea-whip). There are about 35 seahorse species around the world. The larger central one here is from the Caribbean, while the two smaller yellow seahorses live around the Indian and Pacific Oceans. However colour is no accurate guide, for most seahorses can change hues in minutes, from black or grey to bright yellow or orange. The seahorse hunts mainly by sight, sucking tiny water creatures such as baby fishes and shellfish into its tubular mouth. Its eyes turn independently to view two scenes at once - one eye searching for food, perhaps, while the other checks out a possible predator. The seahorse can remain still for long periods, secured by its prehensile tail and well camouflaged among weeds or corals. Only its swivelling eyes may give it away.

Jointed bony rings

Tube-like sucking mouth

PREGNANT FATHER

As the breeding season approaches the male seahorse's pouch, in the front of his lower abdomen, becomes swollen and ready to receive eggs. The female lays up to 200 eggs in the pouch, through her long egg-laying tube (ovipositor). About two to six weeks later the eggs have developed into baby seahorses, ready to be born.

1 The male seahorse grasps a seaweed stem with his curly tail. The opening to the pouch has enlarged slightly, and the babies are moving about inside.

2 He bends his body backwards and forwards, as though suffering from cramp. The pouch opening widens and a baby seahorse shoots out. It rises to the surface and takes a gulp of air, to fill its swim bladder.

3 With continuing convulsions, more baby seahorses are born, in batches of five or so. Each is about 1 cm (.39 in) long, and soon starts feeding on tiny water creatures. The father is very tired by the end of the birth session, which can last two days.

WEEDY HORSE

Australasia's weedy or leafy seadragon is one of the largest seahorses, growing to more than 30 cm (12 in) in length. It is festooned with fleshy flaps and weed-like trailers, making it extremely difficult to spot in its favoured haunt of shallow, seaweed-filled bays. It lacks the prehensile tail of other seahorses and is also a weak swimmer, often found cast ashore after storms. The male guards about 100 eggs at a time in his pouch.

SPOT THE PIPEFISH

The pipefish's long, thin shape and banded greeny-brown colour give it excellent camouflage among the wracks, eelgrasses, and other long, slim seaweeds around the shore. Like seahorses, pipefishes often swim and rest in an upright posture, matching the strands of weed. Although it looks soft and vulnerable, this fish's body has a tough outer case which limits its writhing movements. The male keeps the eggs in a pouch formed by two long flaps of soft skin along his lower abdomen. Even after the babies hatch, they may dash back to the safety of the father's pouch when they sense danger.

TOGETHERNESS

The male and female pipefishes court by swimming upright past each other. Then he rubs her abdomen with his snout several times. Eventually they intertwine and she deposits the eggs in his pouch. Unlike the male seahorse, the pipefish's brood pouch literally bursts to release the young.

Resting in an upright position, the pipefish is well hidden amongst the seaweeds

Pipefish

Small pectoral fin

Long, tube-like snout

Changing faces

THERE ARE ABOUT 520 species in the flatfish group, but none of them are born flat. Upon hatching, they swim upright near the sea surface and look much like any other larval fish. But within a few weeks, remarkable changes take place, known as metamorphosis (change in body form). The larval flatfish's body becomes very thin from side to side. The eye on one side moves over the top of the head to sit next to the eye on the other side. This leaves one side of the fish "blind", but it does not matter, for the blind side becomes the underside. The little fish sinks to the bottom, and the seabed becomes its domain. For the rest of its life, the adult flatfish lies on its blind side.

SOLE SEARCHING

The flatfish shown metamorphosing here is a European or common sole, which grows up to 60 cm (24 in) long. It is probably the most plentiful member of the sole family in European waters. Also known as the Dover sole, this fish spends its days partly buried in the sand, or gravel of the seabed.

1 THREE DAYS OLD
This side view of the baby sole, three days after hatching, shows a fairly normal-looking larval fish. The backbone is in its early stage of development, and a few pigment cells have formed on the otherwise transparent body.
Actual size: 3.5 mm (.14 in)

Yolk sac still visible

Eye

2 FIVE DAYS OLD
The sole's left eye can be seen as a shadowy spot on the other side of the head. At this stage the larval flatfish is still foraging in the upper waters of the sea, where the eggs hatched, and is living off the nutrients in its yolk sac.
Actual size: 3.5 mm (.14 in)

Vertebrae begin to form

3 EIGHT DAYS OLD
More pigment cells grow in the skin, and the skull, jaw bones, and backbone develop further. In a bony fish the shape of the skeleton forms first in cartilage, which gradually hardens (ossifies) into true bone.
Actual size: 3.8 mm (.15 in)

Pigment cells

Backbone is further developed

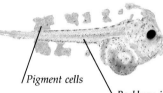

Skin pigment cells merge to form blotches of dark colour

NEARLY A YEARLING
This sole, approaching its first birthday, shows its changeable skin coloration under a mosaic patterning of ctenoid (comb-edged) scales.

Skull has grown more quickly on the left

11 FORTY-FIVE DAYS
Nearly seven weeks after hatching, the sole is its parent in miniature. Skin pigment cells merge to form larger patches and blotches of dark colour. Now the young sole can take to the bottom-dwelling life it will follow when adult. Of the half million or so eggs released by the female parent, very few reach this stage. Even fewer, perhaps only one or two, will grow into mature adults.
Actual size: 11 mm (.43 in)

DISAPPEARING EYES
Young Californian blind gobies have small eyes and can see. But as they grow, the eyes disappear under the skin. This shore-dwelling fish lives in dark crevices and shellfish tunnels.

10 THIRTY-FIVE DAYS
Metamorphosis is almost complete. The skull has grown more quickly on the left, causing this side to enlarge and so swing the left eye over to the right. By this age the young sole has drifted from the spawning ground into the coastal shallows.
Actual size: 10 mm (.39 in)

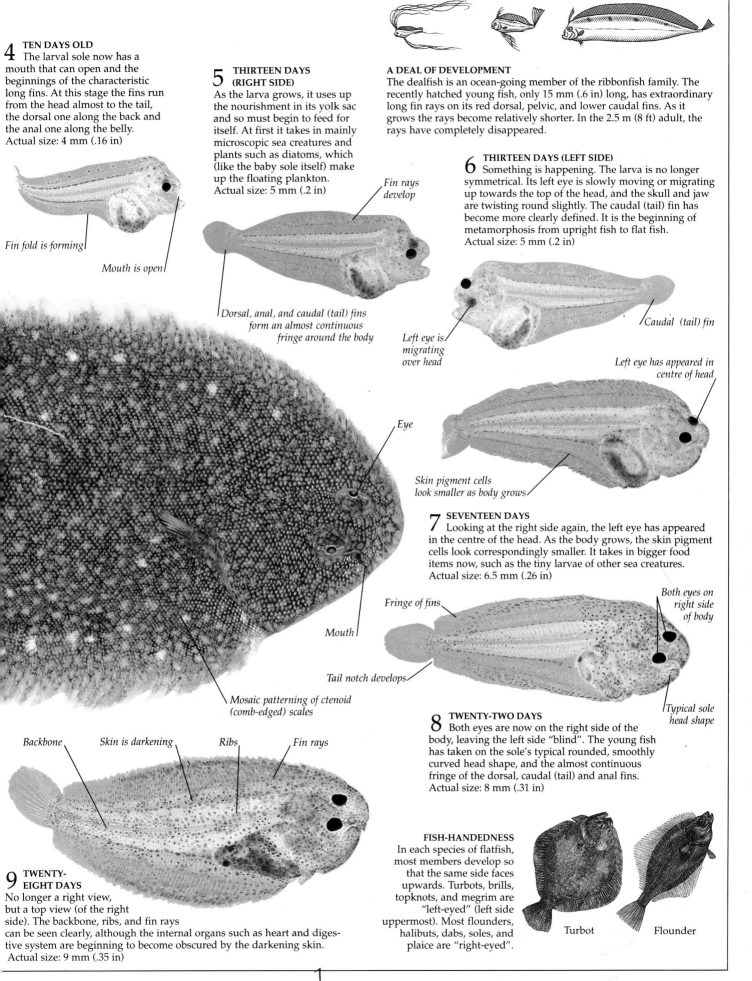

4 TEN DAYS OLD

The larval sole now has a mouth that can open and the beginnings of the characteristic long fins. At this stage the fins run from the head almost to the tail, the dorsal one along the back and the anal one along the belly.
Actual size: 4 mm (.16 in)

Fin fold is forming

Mouth is open

5 THIRTEEN DAYS (RIGHT SIDE)

As the larva grows, it uses up the nourishment in its yolk sac and so must begin to feed for itself. At first it takes in mainly microscopic sea creatures and plants such as diatoms, which (like the baby sole itself) make up the floating plankton.
Actual size: 5 mm (.2 in)

Fin rays develop

Dorsal, anal, and caudal (tail) fins form an almost continuous fringe around the body

A DEAL OF DEVELOPMENT

The dealfish is an ocean-going member of the ribbonfish family. The recently hatched young fish, only 15 mm (.6 in) long, has extraordinary long fin rays on its red dorsal, pelvic, and lower caudal fins. As it grows the rays become relatively shorter. In the 2.5 m (8 ft) adult, the rays have completely disappeared.

6 THIRTEEN DAYS (LEFT SIDE)

Something is happening. The larva is no longer symmetrical. Its left eye is slowly moving or migrating up towards the top of the head, and the skull and jaw are twisting round slightly. The caudal (tail) fin has become more clearly defined. It is the beginning of metamorphosis from upright fish to flat fish.
Actual size: 5 mm (.2 in)

Left eye is migrating over head

Caudal (tail) fin

Left eye has appeared in centre of head

Skin pigment cells look smaller as body grows

Eye

Mouth

Mosaic patterning of ctenoid (comb-edged) scales

7 SEVENTEEN DAYS

Looking at the right side again, the left eye has appeared in the centre of the head. As the body grows, the skin pigment cells look correspondingly smaller. It takes in bigger food items now, such as the tiny larvae of other sea creatures.
Actual size: 6.5 mm (.26 in)

Fringe of fins

Both eyes on right side of body

Tail notch develops

Typical sole head shape

8 TWENTY-TWO DAYS

Both eyes are now on the right side of the body, leaving the left side "blind". The young fish has taken on the sole's typical rounded, smoothly curved head shape, and the almost continuous fringe of the dorsal, caudal (tail) and anal fins.
Actual size: 8 mm (.31 in)

Backbone   *Skin is darkening*   *Ribs*   *Fin rays*

9 TWENTY-EIGHT DAYS

No longer a right view, but a top view (of the right side). The backbone, ribs, and fin rays can be seen clearly, although the internal organs such as heart and digestive system are beginning to become obscured by the darkening skin.
Actual size: 9 mm (.35 in)

FISH-HANDEDNESS

In each species of flatfish, most members develop so that the same side faces upwards. Turbots, brills, topknots, and megrim are "left-eyed" (left side uppermost). Most flounders, halibuts, dabs, soles, and plaice are "right-eyed".

Turbot   Flounder

Continued on next page

Flat fishes

Like most flatfishes, the plaice lives on or near the seabed, well camouflaged by its spotty coloration. It swims by flapping its entire body up and down with a wave-like motion. Then it stiffens and glides down to land on the bottom. Here it swishes its fins to brush up mud, sand, or gravel. The particles settle back over the fish's body and partly cover it, breaking up its outline and making it even more difficult to spot.

Zig-zag muscle blocks (flesh) visible on underside of plaice

Left pectoral fin

WHITE SIDE DOWN
The plaice is a "right-eyed" flatfish, keeping its blind left side flat against the seabed. Since this side is not normally visible, the fish saves the effort involved in making and maintaining skin pigment cells. This means the underside is natural flesh-coloured white or cream. However, a few plaice have their undersides pigmented also, a condition known as ambicoloration. Small scales are embedded in the skin and the "blind" left side of the mouth has more teeth than the upper side.

Lower gill cover

Pelvic fin

Upper gill cover

Eyes are on right side

PLAICE FACE
As this front view shows, flatfishes are not truly flat. The upper side is more rounded than the lower one, to give a low humped shape. During metamorphosis, the plaice's mouth twists only slightly from its original position.

Small scales embedded in skin

Spotty coloration changes according to background

26

White underside is not normally visible

Blood vessels visible

Caudal fin (tail)

Eyes face upwards on lemon sole skeleton

FLAT SKELETON

At first sight, this could be the skeleton of a deep-bodied, disc-shaped fish that swam upright in the normal way. The hole at the front below the head is for the heart and other main internal organs. But a closer look at the head reveals two eyes facing right – or rather upwards. For this is the skeleton of a lemon sole, a type of flatfish. Compare it with the cod skeleton on page 10. The backbone, ribs, and fin rays all correspond, although their proportions differ somewhat. Only the front of the head is twisted. Confusingly, the lemon sole is not a true sole, but more closely related to the dab and plaice.

Spots from back showing through on underside

CHAMELEON FISH

As flatfishes evolved to forsake speed and take up a more inactive life on the seabed, they became easier meals for predators. So they also evolved the ability to change skin pattern and colour, to blend in with different backgrounds as they moved about. Blending camouflage also helps them to remain unnoticed by their own prey - until the last second. Colours change under the control of nerves and hormones. Each skin pigment cell (chromatophore) has fine branches into which it can spread its pigment grains; this colours its tiny patch of skin. If the grains are drawn tightly into the centre of the cell, the background colour shows through.

Flounder

Turbot

Plaice

THE FLAT FAMILY

Flatfishes all have one thing in common - their flatness, but they vary in size and habitat. The flounder, about 50 cm (20 in) long, can live in the sea or in fresh water. The turbot, a left-eyed flatfish, grows to 1 m (3 ft) and eats mainly other fishes. The plaice is smaller, usually around 50 cm (20 in). Soles live in shallow coastal waters and hunt for food at night. Dab larvae move to depths of up to 70 m (230 ft) before becoming "flat".

Sole

Dab

The art of swimming

IF YOU CAN "SWIM LIKE A FISH" it means that you have mastered the art of swimming, something that comes naturally to fishes. They swim like snakes wriggle: by a series of S-shaped curves, or "waves", that travel along the body. Each wave begins with a small sideways motion of the head, but becomes bigger as it sweeps along the body, so that the tail moves much further sideways. The body and tail push the surrounding water sideways and backwards, and so propel the fish forwards. In most fishes the tail produces a large amount of the total forward thrust, but some species "row" with their pectoral fins rather than using the tail. Each S-shaped wave is produced by contractions of muscle blocks on either side of the backbone. Each muscle block or myotome contracts a split second after the one in front of it, pulling that side of the body around into a curve which forms the wave. In a steadily swimming dogfish there is about one complete wave each second.

TALE OF THE WHALE
The tail of a whale is horizontal, unlike the vertical tail (caudal fin) of a fish. A whale swims by arching its body up and down, rather than from side to side as in a fish. Whales such as the humpback can accelerate under water and hurl their 50 tons of bulk clear of the surface, to fall back with an enormous splash. This is called "breaching".

Caudal fin (tail)

Second dorsal fin

Spotty coloration

First dorsal fin

"S" FOR SWIMMING
In this sequence of photographs, which covers about one second of time, the S-shaped wave of movement passes along the body of the dogfish and is "thrown off" by the tail. To begin new waves the head swings slightly, first to one side and then the other, which propels the fish forwards (the left and right sideways tail and body movements cancel out). Compared to species such as the eels, the dogfish does not have a very flexible body.

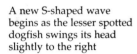

A new S-shaped wave begins as the lesser spotted dogfish swings its head slightly to the right

The "peak" of the wave has passed along the body to between the pectoral and pelvic fins

The peak has now travelled to the region of the pelvic and first dorsal fins

TOPSY-TURVY FISHES
Many fishes can turn on their sides and even roll right over. But a few can actually swim upside-down quite happily for long periods. They include the upside-down catfish, originally from the Congo region of Africa and now kept in tropical freshwater aquariums around the world. Its mouth is on the under-side of the head, as in other catfishes. This is ideal for grubbing about on the bottom, but not for taking items from the surface. The upside-down catfish has solved the problem by turning right over, so that it can consume flies and other prey that have fallen onto the water's surface.

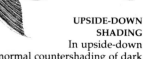

UPSIDE-DOWN SHADING
In upside-down catfishes, the normal countershading of dark back and light underside (p. 18) is missing or even reversed, to give a dark belly and pale back. The aquarium upside-down catfish (left) is about 6 cm (2 in) long. The position of the lateral line when upside-down is shown in a related species (above).

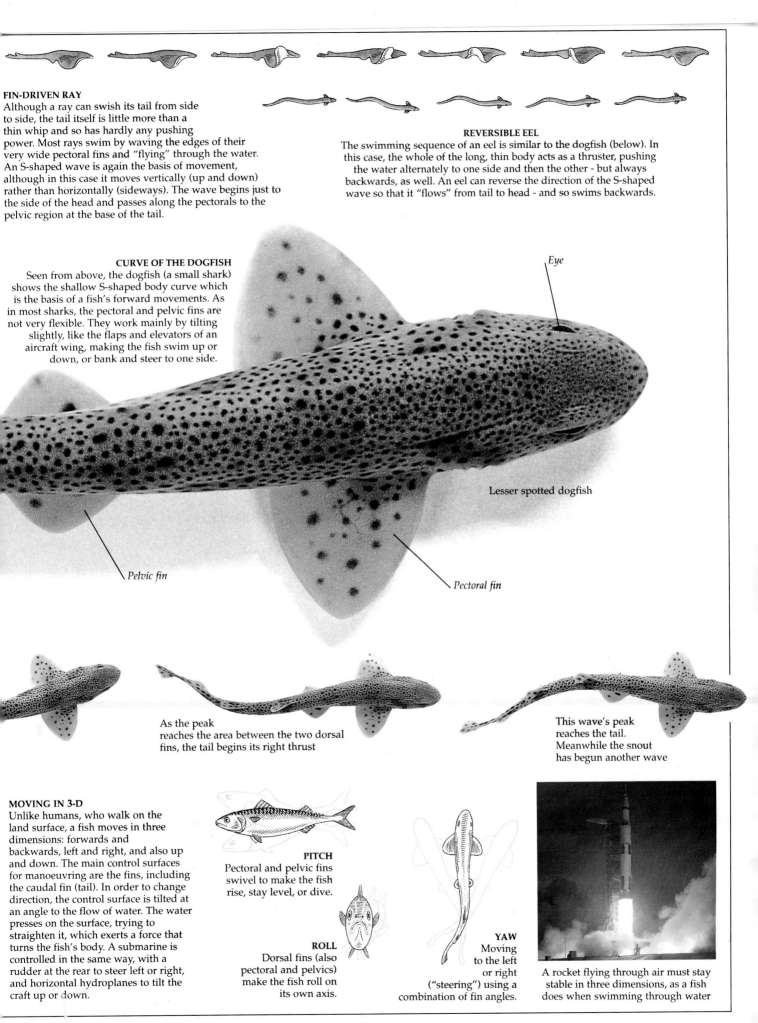

FIN-DRIVEN RAY

Although a ray can swish its tail from side to side, the tail itself is little more than a thin whip and so has hardly any pushing power. Most rays swim by waving the edges of their very wide pectoral fins and "flying" through the water. An S-shaped wave is again the basis of movement, although in this case it moves vertically (up and down) rather than horizontally (sideways). The wave begins just to the side of the head and passes along the pectorals to the pelvic region at the base of the tail.

REVERSIBLE EEL

The swimming sequence of an eel is similar to the dogfish (below). In this case, the whole of the long, thin body acts as a thruster, pushing the water alternately to one side and then the other - but always backwards, as well. An eel can reverse the direction of the S-shaped wave so that it "flows" from tail to head - and so swims backwards.

CURVE OF THE DOGFISH

Seen from above, the dogfish (a small shark) shows the shallow S-shaped body curve which is the basis of a fish's forward movements. As in most sharks, the pectoral and pelvic fins are not very flexible. They work mainly by tilting slightly, like the flaps and elevators of an aircraft wing, making the fish swim up or down, or bank and steer to one side.

Eye

Lesser spotted dogfish

Pelvic fin

Pectoral fin

As the peak reaches the area between the two dorsal fins, the tail begins its right thrust

This wave's peak reaches the tail. Meanwhile the snout has begun another wave

MOVING IN 3-D

Unlike humans, who walk on the land surface, a fish moves in three dimensions: forwards and backwards, left and right, and also up and down. The main control surfaces for manoeuvring are the fins, including the caudal fin (tail). In order to change direction, the control surface is tilted at an angle to the flow of water. The water presses on the surface, trying to straighten it, which exerts a force that turns the fish's body. A submarine is controlled in the same way, with a rudder at the rear to steer left or right, and horizontal hydroplanes to tilt the craft up or down.

PITCH
Pectoral and pelvic fins swivel to make the fish rise, stay level, or dive.

ROLL
Dorsal fins (also pectoral and pelvics) make the fish roll on its own axis.

YAW
Moving to the left or right ("steering") using a combination of fin angles.

A rocket flying through air must stay stable in three dimensions, as a fish does when swimming through water

Tails and fins

A FISH'S FINS are a compromise between moving and staying still. Most fishes propel themselves with their fins, especially the caudal fin (tail); yet at the same time they must be able to steer and stop accurately, doing this with their pectoral, dorsal, and pelvic fins. It is possible to guess a fish's way of life from the shape of its fins. Slim, knife-like side fins and a narrow, deeply forked tail indicate a fast cruiser, as in the tuna or sailfish. Relatively large, broad side fins and a wide, square-ended tail aid manoeuvring and are found in slow swimmers that live near the bottom and among rocks and reefs.

Sailfish tail

SAIL TAIL
The sailfish (p.10) is one of the fastest of all fishes, with speeds estimated at more than 96 kph (60 mph). The crescent-shaped or "lunate" tail, narrow yet deep, is typical of fishes that cruise at high speed. It has little flesh and few scales, being made chiefly of fin rays. The tail is only slightly flexible, but is incredibly strong, to transmit the enormous power of the body muscles through to the water.

Tail is crescent-shaped for speed

KINGFISH FINS
The kingfish's round body shape is not at all streamlined, but the long fins extending from its body make it easier to move fast through the water.

ON TIPTOE
Enormous pectoral fins and plenty of spiny fin rays make the tub gurnard an extremely prickly fish. The first three rays of each pectoral fin are separate, and move to and fro like spider's legs as the gurnard "tiptoes" along the seabed.

Soft edge to sucker seals to host skin

Remora sucker

Plates in sucker tilt to create a vacuum

STUCK ON SHARKS
The remora has evolved a dorsal fin that acts as a powerful sucker. It often sticks to a blue shark, hitching a ride and feeding on the host's parasites, and perhaps sharing in any leftovers.

Long upper lobe turns upwards on fish

UNEQUAL LOBES
The uneven-looking sturgeon tail is heterocercal – a type also sported by many sharks. The fish's backbone turns upwards into the upper lobe, and most of the rays that form the two lobes of the tail fin come from the backbone's underside. The rays from the upper side of the backbone form only the small topmost part of the tail.

UNLIKELY TAIL
The butterfly fish tail is hardly divided into two lobes at all. This specimen caught in East Africa bore scrawls that resembled, presumably by chance, old Arabic writing which translates as: "There is no God but Allah". Consequently, it fetched a hefty price at the fish market!

Fin rays

Sturgeon tail

FUSED TAIL
In some species of armoured catfishes, the upper and lower lobes of the tail fin are joined to form one large fin surface. The twin notches give the tail a "double emarginate" outline.

Butterfly fish tail

لا إله إلا الله

Notch on tail fin

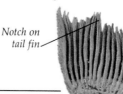

Armoured catfish tail

FISH SHOULDER
The bases of the pectoral fins are linked to the body by the bones of the pectoral girdle, which can be compared to human shoulder joints. This is the pectoral girdle of the upside-down catfish, which sculls along with its large fins (p. 28). The fin spines can be locked rigidly upright.

Fin rays are loaded with poison in life

DEATH RAY
In life, the long, slender fin rays of the lionfish are loaded with deadly poison (p. 55). The rays are highly coloured and mostly separate, rather than being joined by the usual web-like fin membrane.

Rays of fin fan out when fish is in flight

ON THE WING
Flying fishes leap from the water and glide (rather than fly) on their long pectoral fins. The fins fold against the body when swimming, but as the fish takes off the rays are opened out in a fan-like fashion to give a good area for the "wing".

Flying fishes in flight above the water surface

Interlocking ring in back

Ring at base of spine

Fin spine

RAISING RAYS
In many catfishes, the first ray or rays of the dorsal fin have evolved into strong spines that can be raised or lowered on a special joint consisting of two interlocking rings. This is such a joint from a sea catfish. The great bony shield in this fish is also a fin support.

Dorsal spine locked upright

LOCKED UP
The front dorsal spine of the triggerfish can be locked upright by the second "trigger" spine that slots down behind it.

Trigger spine

OPEN EYED
With a sudden swish, the eyed *Pteraclis* raises its hugely expandable dorsal and ventral fins. The fish seems to become enormous and the dark eyespot adds to the predator-startling effect.

Square end of tail fin

CUT-OFF CAUDAL
This broad, square-ended ("truncated") caudal fin indicates a normally slow mover, capable of only the odd dash to safety. Indeed, it belongs to one of the parrot-fishes (p. 35), slow-swimming grazers of coral reefs.

TWO-LOBED CAT
Some armoured catfishes have a distinctly two-lobed caudal fin, each lobe consisting of thickened fin rays to make the tail very strong but none-too-flexible.

Overlapping lobes

Armoured catfish tail

Parrotfish tail

Fishes with legs

NOT SURPRISINGLY, FISHES ARE MAINLY thought of as swimming in water. But there are some kinds of fishes that can "walk", using their fins as "legs", and even leave the water and breathe air for long periods without coming to any harm. Mudskippers, for instance, "skip" across coastal mudflats and mangrove (tropical tree) swamps in Africa, south-east Asia, and Australasia. They breathe by way of an "aqualung", in the form of water kept in their large gill chambers. The gurnard uses the spiny rays of its pectoral fins to creep delicately along the sea bottom (p. 30). Some African catfishes elbow their way across dry land much like the mudskippers, looking a bit like combat soldiers crawling on their chests. Some fishes can absorb oxygen directly from the air. They gulp it into the mouth and throat, where folds of skin or other special structures have a rich supply of blood vessels which pick up the oxygen. These include the climbing perches, which have been found in trees!

FINS LIKE OARS
Blennies have strong pectoral fins, which can be used as oars to "row" across bare rock when stranded out of water in their rocky shore habitat. This blenny is on the shore, probably on its way to a shallow pool.

LEGLESS FISH
The "fizzigiggious fish", a strange character in an Edward Lear nursery rhyme, always walked on stilts, because he had no legs!

Moist muddy surface

FISH ON STILTS

The curious tripod fish dwells in the dark depths 3,000 m (9,843 ft) below the sea's surface. Its two pelvic fins and the lower lobe of its tail fin are drawn into long stiff filaments. The fish props itself up on these, like stilts, and stands on the ocean bottom.

Tripod fish

Tripod fish can prop itself up on these long stiff filaments

FISHES WITH LUNGS

Fully equipped with lungs as well as gills, lungfishes have survived from 300 million years ago, and can breathe air out of water. The African lungfish (right) has burrowed into the mud at the bottom of a swamp that has dried out during drought. After burrowing, it secretes mucus to form a cocoon which conserves moisture, and breathes through a porous mud plug at the top until the drought is over. The Australian lungfish (below) is literally in a family of its own. Although it rises to the surface to gulp in fresh air, it cannot hibernate to survive drought, and only abandons gill-breathing in adverse conditions.

African lungfish hibernating in mud burrow during a drought

Australian lungfish

A WALK IN THE MUD

In South-east Asia, in a muddy coastal swamp sweats in the tropical heat. Most water creatures are following the tide down the shore, or burying themselves in the safe dampness of the mud. But here and there, small wedge-shaped, pop-eyed creatures scurry across the moist surface, feeding on insects, attracting mates, and defending their territories. These mudskippers (below) can prop themselves up and skip quickly on their muscular pectoral fins, which look like stubby crutches. They can also leap along the mud, and can often be seen playfully leaping about in chase of each other.

Mangrove trunks

A thick layer of clear skin protects bulging eyes

To keep eyes moist out of water, mudskippers can roll them back into the moist sockets

Short muscular pectoral fins look like stubby little legs out of water

Dorsal fin

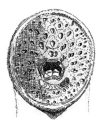

Fishes feeding

"BIG FISHES EAT little fishes, and little fishes eat even smaller fishes . . . but what do these even smaller fishes eat?". This old question was soon solved when naturalists could look through a magnifying lens. Life in water, as on land, is based on plants. Most plants in the sea are microscopic and floating, and are called the phytoplankton. Tiny floating animals called zooplankton eat them; small creatures such as shrimps eat the plankton; and so the grand food web of life continues. The front end of a fish gives many clues to its diet. Large, crushing teeth indicate meals of shellfish, corals, or tough plant matter; sharp, pointed teeth indicate a hunting lifestyle; while a wide, gaping mouth shows a gulping method of feeding.

THE BLOODSUCKER
One of the few jawless fishes, the lamprey feeds by attaching itself to its prey with a sucker, then rasping away at its flesh with its teeth, and sucking its blood.

SKEWERED FISH
The popular notion of a swordfish with an unfortunate victim impaled on its sword is shown in this fanciful engraving.

Elephant-snout fish skull

Tiny jaws at end of "nose"

POKING ITS NOSE IN
The elephant-snout fish from Africa has a long, curved "nose" with tiny jaws at the end. It pokes these between stones, into cracks and down into the mud, to find its food of small water creatures.

Pouting mouth for sucking in food

Porcupine fish skull

European bream skull

SURPRISING JAWS
The European John Dory has a surprise in store for unwary prey. Deep-bodied but extremely thin, this fish creeps up on smaller fishes and prawns, keeping head on to make itself look inconspicuous. Then its great jaws suddenly lever forward and engulf the prey.

John Dory skull

CHEWING THROAT
The common or European bream, a silvery-olive freshwater fish, has a "pouting" mouth which it uses to sift and churn through the mud, sucking up small bottom-dwelling worms, shellfish, and insect larvae. These are then ground up by pharyngeal or throat teeth.

Pharyngeal teeth of bream

PRICKLES NO PROBLEM
The porcupine fish is well known for the ability to puff itself up and erect its spines when threatened (p. 38). Lesser known is its diet, which consists of hard-shelled mussels and other shellfish, corals lurking in their stony homes, and even sea-urchins hiding beneath their own spines. In each jaw, the teeth are fused to form a hard-edged biting ridge at the front, with a flat crushing plate behind.

FRUIT AND NUT CASE
The pacu, from the Amazon region of Brazil, eats fruits and nuts which fall into the river. Its strong, crushing teeth are at the front of its mouth, for biting and gathering food.

Strong, crushing teeth

Prawn

Hard-shelled mussels

Seed of *Pirhanea trifoliata* (the piranha tree)

Brazil nuts

TRUMPETFISH TWEEZERS
A long, rigid "beak" extends between the trumpetfish's small mouth and its eyes. The snout and the tiny teeth at the end are used like tweezers, to winkle small aquatic animals out of their hidey holes.

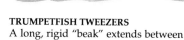

BEWARE THE BARRACUDA

Fearsome predators of warmer oceans, barracudas seize, maim, and tear up other fishes with their formidable array of spear-like teeth. The larger barracudas, which grow to nearly 3 m (12 ft) long, have been known to attack humans. However, many divers say the barracudas do not deserve their bad reputation. Although they may trail humans for some time, and they certainly look frightening enough, they rarely strike unless provoked.

Sharp, dagger-like teeth

Sharp triangular teeth lock together for a clean bite

MOUTHFUL OF FANGS

The South American piranha or piraya has a mouthful of triangular, blade-like teeth. This river fish eats fruit and seeds as well as other fishes. A group can soon devour larger prey by neatly chopping it into bits.

STONY FACED

The wide, upward-facing mouth of the stonefish gulps in unwary prey as it lies on the seabed, camouflaged by its remarkably rock-like appearance.

Wide mouth on top of head

Stonefish skull

SHARP NOSE

Not a medieval sword, but the nose of the spectacular swordfish. The entire fish may be more than 4 m (14 ft) long; youngsters have a relatively short bill (snout) which lengthens into the flattened sword as they mature. No-one is sure exactly what the sword is used for. It may strike prey fishes, or impale them, or simply be a result of extreme streamlining, the sword making the fish's progress faster.

CORAL CRUSHERS COMBINED

Coral reefs harbour an amazing variety of fishes, which have a similarly amazing variety of feeding methods. The powerful, horny "beak" of the parrotfish is made of fused teeth. It scrapes the thin layer of algae (seaweeds) and corals from rocks; the food is then ground to a powder by strong pharyngeal plates. The drawn-out snout of the forceps fish (p. 16) is ideal for inserting into crannies and nooks for small bits of food. Both the triggerfish and the leather jacket's chisel-like teeth can bore holes in shells.

Horny beak

Parrotfish skull

Leather jacket skull

Coral

Triggerfish skull

Forceps fish skull

Swordfish nose

SURFACE SKIMMER

Called the halfbeak because the lower jaw is usually longer than the upper, this fish skims the undersurface of the water, swallowing plankton and larval fishes.

CHAINSAW MASSACRE

This partly cutaway sawfish snout shows the "blades" of teeth in cartilage sockets. In fact this is a cartilaginous fish, a close relative of the rays. Razor-sharp teeth on the saw can kill fishes. It is also used for probing into the seabed to dislodge food such as molluscs and crustaceans. The biggest sawfishes are over 7 m (24 ft) long.

Sawfish snout

Sharp saw teeth in cartilage sockets

Food out of water

Mᴏꜱᴛ ꜰɪꜱʜᴇꜱ ꜰᴇᴇᴅ in their natural surroundings – water. Some, like trout, rise to the surface to snatch drowning flies and other food, trapped at the surface film or flying just above. But a few fishes are able to catch food which is entirely out of water. The archerfishes are among the most expert. There are some five species of archerfishes, swimming in the tropical mangrove coasts of India and Australasia. Most of the time, the archerfish does not use its "arrows". It feeds on prey swimming or floating in the water. When enticed by hunger, however, this fish can squirt a jet of water droplets at insects and other creatures on the leaves and stems above the surface. The surprise attack knocks the prey into the water, where the archerfish snaps it up.

Spider on leaf is the prey

Butterfly fish

LEAPING BUTTERFLY

The West African butterfly fish swims close to the surface of grassy swamps and snaps up surface-living insects. It can also leap out to catch a tasty morsel, at heights of over 2 m (6 ft) – some feat for a fish no longer than 10 cm (4 in).

Jet of water aimed at the spider

A DIRECT HIT

The archerfish swims slowly to a position just below its victim, looking up with its very large eyes. Then it tilts its body almost vertical, rises so the tip of its snout is just at the surface, and lets fly with a volley of water drops. Shooting almost straight up makes it easier to aim at the target than if the fish shot from the side. If the first volley of droplets misses, the fish can quickly adjust its aim and shoot again, and again. Archerfishes begin to "spit" when very young, although they seem to do this largely at random and the jets only travel about 10 cm (4 in). As they get older, distance and aim improve. An experienced adult can score a direct hit on a victim more than 1.5 m (5 ft) above the water's surface.

THE ARCHER'S WATER-JET PUMP

When the archerfish is ready to "shoot", it snaps shut its gill covers, which compresses water in the gill chambers and mouth. The tongue presses upwards against a groove in the roof of the mouth, turning this into a tube which produces a fast, narrow stream of water.

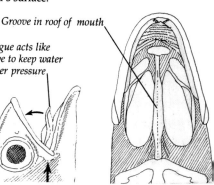

Groove in roof of mouth

Tongue acts like valve to keep water under pressure

Side view of archerfish's mouth showing movement of tongue

Inside view of roof of archerfish's mouth

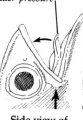

Spider on leaf is about to be snapped up by archerfish

LEAPING FOR ITS SUPPER

Archerfishes not only shoot at prey, they can also leap out of the water and knock it down. In an aquarium, they may jump up at food stuck to the side of the glass, 30 cm (12 in) above the surface. They have also been seen to leap at and catch low-flying insects. However, it is not success every time. Archerfishes jump or squirt at inedible objects, such as marks on the aquarium glass or curious people leaning over to watch them. They often seem to shoot when they see a person blink, which is one in the eye for the observer! In the wild, these fishes prefer brackish (salty) waters in estuaries, but they will swim up rivers into fresh water. They lay their eggs on near-shore rocks and coral reefs.

AERIAL HUNTER

Deep in the Amazon rainforest lurks the arawana, a slim and agile fish with a cavernous, scoop-like mouth. It feeds on water creatures such as shellfish and small crabs, and it may take small snakes too. And, like the archerfish, the arawana can leap clear of the water in an attempt to catch an insect, small bird, or bat just above. These antics have earned it the local name of "water monkey".

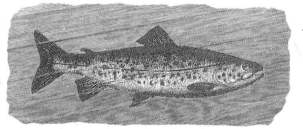

CRAFTY OLD TROUT

Trouts often rise to the surface to feed on drowning flies or other food trapped at the surface.

Scaring the enemy

LIGHT FOR LIFE
Many deep-sea fishes have luminous organs which can protect them from predators by either making them seem to "disappear", or by blinding them, like car headlights. This scaled dragon fish has luminous chin barbels.

IN THE UNDERWATER world, fishes are always ready to deal with an enemy – usually a predator on the prowl. A burst of speed is one way to foil the hunters. Size is another, since very big fishes are too much of a mouthful, while very small ones can take refuge in cracks and crevices. Yet another tactic is camouflage (p. 50). However, some fishes have evolved devious weapons to defend themselves from hungry hunters. The porcupine and pufferfishes, for example, can make themselves swell up and erect their prickles or spines to discourage feeders. Triggerfishes have a spine on the back which can be locked erect by a bony projection of the smaller second spine. As a triggerfish struggles, its rigid spine can inflict great damage to a predator.

THE SURGEON'S SCALPEL
Surgeonfishes are colourful inhabitants of coral reefs throughout the tropical Pacific. The name comes from a sharp, bony, blade-like "lancet" on either side of the body, near the base of the tail. These blades cut flesh as cleanly as a surgeon's scalpel. In some species there is a row of small blades; in others the lancets lie folded in a groove when not in use, but can be flicked out for use, like flick knives, as the fish suddenly turns and thrashes its tail at an enemy. Surgeonfishes use their razors mainly for defence, lashing out at predators. Most of the time they graze among the coral and weeds, rowing along with their pectoral fins.

Surgeonfish

Pectoral fins

Tall, thin, deep-bodied shape

Long anal fin

Lancet blade

Lancet blade extended at right angles to the fish

Spines lie flat along body when porcupine fish is at rest

GOING UP

The porcupine fish is the hedgehog of the fish world. Like a hedgehog, it can erect its spines to make a prickly mouthful that puts off potential predators. Unlike a hedgehog, however, the porcupine fish can also inflate its body like a balloon, becoming far too large for the average predator to swallow. There are several species of porcupine fishes, which live in mainly tropical seas. Close relatives are the pufferfishes, which have a similar ability to blow themselves up. A deflated or "relaxed" porcupine fish (above) looks much like many other fishes, although it has rather prominent eyes. As soon as danger approaches, this fish quickly swallows water and balloons to two or three times its normal size. If a porcupine fish is taken from the water suddenly, it can take in air instead of water to inflate in the same way. When the danger is past, the fish slowly lets itself down again.

Spines swivel out to stand at right angles to body when porcupine fish is inflated

Pale underside colour is more pronounced than when deflated

Normal (deflated) shape of pufferfish

Pufferfish inflated to full extent to intimidate enemy

OUT OF PUFF
These before-and-after views of a pufferfish show how the length of the fish remains unchanged after puffing up.

Setting up house

Youngsters at the seaside: a black goby watches over its hatchlings

LIKE OTHER BABY animals, baby fishes develop from the eggs of the female, fertilized by the male. On land, mother and father must come together to mate. But in fishes, it is often enough for them to be near each other, since the water in which they live brings the eggs and sperm together. Thousands of fish species gather in the breeding season and spawn (lay and fertilize eggs) by simply shedding their roe (eggs) and milt (sperm) into the same patch of water. However, some species have courtship routines, usually where the male attracts the female with his bright breeding colours. Setting up a nest and guarding it, as in the three-spined stickleback, is another way to give eggs and young a greater chance of survival.

NEST AT SEA
The male 15-spined or sea stickleback makes a nest, like its freshwater cousin. Small bits of seaweeds are positioned in a larger clump and then "roped" together by a sticky thread produced by the male's kidneys.

RED AND BLUE BREEDERS
Every spring, in ponds, lakes, and rivers across the Northern Hemisphere, three-spined sticklebacks prepare to breed. Each male develops a splendid deep-red throat and chest, and bright blue eyes. He chases off other red-throated males and stakes out his territory - his own patch of water. Here he will build a nest, entice a female to lay eggs in it, fertilize them, guard them as they develop, and watch over the young as they hatch and grow.

Piece of water plant stickleback's mouth f the nest

Bright blue eye

Red thro

1 COLLECTING THE MATERIALS
The male stickleback sets about collecting little bits of water plants for the nest.

Beneath a sma boulder is th ideal site o which t build a nes

Stickleba shovels grav with his sno

2 DIGGING THE FOUNDATION
He pushes his snout into the stones and mud of the bottom, shovelling them aside to make a shallow hole. The nest is often situated among water weeds or in the shelter of a small boulder.

3 A FIRM BASE
As the male begins to push plant pieces into place, he taps and prods them firmly to make a secure base. The large fan-like pectoral fins come in useful for the precise manoeuvring that this process requires.

Stickleba makes a fir base by proddin weeds into pla with his sno

4 CEMENT STAGE

As the pile of nest material grows, the male cements it together with sticky "glue" - a secretion made by specialized parts of his kidneys. Gradually the nest grows, layer by layer.

BLOWING BUBBLES FOR BABIES

The dwarf gourami, like many of its relatives, is a bubble-nest breeder. The male, resplendent in its breeding colours of shining turquoise and red stripes, lures the female to lay eggs. Then he fertilizes them and blows them into a mass of floating saliva-coated bubbles, where they begin their development.

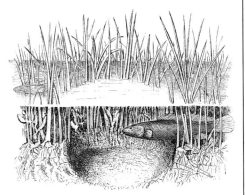

5 ADDED VENTILATION

The collection of weeds and glue prevent a good flow of fresh water through the nest, which will be needed to keep the eggs well aerated. So the fish uses his large fins to fan a current of water through the nest.

Fan-like pectoral fins create a current of water to aerate the nest

PATERNAL INSTINCT

The bowfin is a holostean fish (p. 9) from eastern North America. Each spring the male makes a rough scoop of gravel, roots and other plant pieces, usually in a swampy part of his lake or river home. One or more females lay eggs, which the male fertilizes and then guards until the larvae hatch. These stick themselves into the nest by glue-glands on their heads, feeding off their yolk sacs (p. 42) until they can swim freely.

Mouth agape in "yawn"

"Yawn" display

STICKLEBACK AT WORK

As the male selects his site and begins construction, he stops occasionally over the nest and performs short actions like those above. This is thought to advertize to other fishes that building is in progress, so keep away!

"S-bend" display

COMPLICATED COURTING

Like the male stickleback, the male dragonet (a European inshore fish) intensifies his colours and displays his alluring body and fins to the female. He is about 30 cm (12 in) long; she is two-thirds this size and duller in colour. He attracts her with excited circling and other courting movements, then the two pair up and swim together, with their anal fins forming a channel through which eggs and sperm are released. After all this complicated activity, the parents swim off and leave the eggs to hatch on their own.

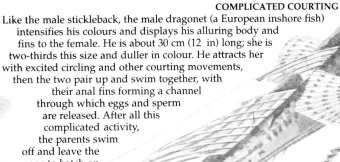

Male and female dragonet pair, ready to release eggs and sperm

Fish eggs

Genuine black caviar
(from beluga sturgeon)

Red caviar (from
salmon) may
be dyed black
during processing

EGG ON TOAST
A few types of fish eggs, or roe, have become delicacies for the human palate - in the form of caviar. People consume them partly for their taste, and also because of their scarcity value. Sadly the fishing of mature females for caviar, even if they are put back afterwards, is threatening the future of several species, especially the huge beluga sturgeon.

As a group, fishes show almost the full range of breeding methods. Species such as cod and turbot release tiny eggs in their millions, scattering them in the water to become fertilized and develop unaided. All but a handful of the millions will soon end up as food for water creatures. On the other hand, the bullhead lays only one or two hundred eggs, and the male guards them fiercely as the embryos (babies) inside develop and hatch into fry. These are all oviparous species – that is, the eggs develop outside the body. Not all fishes lay eggs, however. Some species, especially sharks, are viviparous, like mammals. This means that the embryos grow inside the mother's body and she gives birth to fully formed young.

UNDER THE THUMB
In the springtime, "pincushions" of up to 250 round, yellowish eggs appear in stony scoops along the bottoms of shallow rivers and gravelly lakes. These are egg masses of the female bullhead, or miller's thumb - so-called since its broad, flat head apparently resembles the wide thumb of the miller, who always tested flour and grain by rolling it between finger and thumb. The male bullhead guards and fans the eggs for up to a month as they hatch and the young begin to swim. However any later leavers from the nest are eaten by their father!

Round, yellowish
clump of eggs

Broad, flat head gives
miller's thumb its name

INSIDE THE EGG

These are the eggs of the three-spined stickleback (p. 40), seven days after fertilization, as seen under a low-power microscope. In life they are about 2 mm (.07 in) across, and take from 5 to 12 days to hatch, depending on the temperature of the water. The developing embryo inside lives on food reserves contained in a bulbous, yellowish yolk sac as its organs form. When they hatch, the young or fry will be about 4 mm (.16 in) long.

Dogfish embryo

Dogfish and her egg cases

BORN FROM A PURSE

The hard, horny "mermaid's purses" often washed up on the beach are usually the dried-out, empty egg cases of dogfishes, skates, and rays. The male fertilizes the eggs within the female's body. These begin to develop, then she lays them in pairs in their egg cases, attached to seaweeds by long, curly tendrils at each corner. The embryos grow inside, living on the yolk sac. After 6 to 9 months they wriggle out at around 10 cm (4 in) long.

Wide pectoral fins ideal for fanning and aerating the eggs

Chimaera egg case

CASE COLLECTION

Egg cases vary according to the type of fish that lays them. The chimaera (p. 20) produces a long tadpole-like case; that of the bottom-dwelling Port Jackson shark from Australia is a distinctive corkscrew shape; while the spotted ray's case conforms more to the common "mermaid's purse" outline.

Port Jackson shark egg case

Spotted ray egg case

Miller's thumb guarding clumps of eggs on rock

MUSSEL NURSERY

One of the most unusual egg-laying places is in the freshwater mussel, a shellfish living in lakes and slow rivers. At spawning time in late spring, the female bitterling grows a long tube known as an ovipositor, through which she lays her eggs into the body cavity of the mussel. The male releases his sperm nearby and the mussel sucks this in as it filter-feeds. The male may then stand guard as the eggs develop and young hatch out, eventually swimming free from their shellfish nursery a month later.

Attentive parents

SOME FISHES seem to lack the maternal instinct. They release millions of eggs into the water and happily swim away, leaving them at the mercy of nature (p. 42). But others show themselves to be remarkably caring parents. Mouthbrooders, as the word suggests, refers to fishes like the cichlids that care for their eggs and young in their mouth and throat cavities. The female usually carries out this task. The male sea catfish does a similar job. Seahorse and pipefish fathers (p. 22) brood the eggs and some kinds protect their young. Even the sharks (p. 58), which normally attack any prey including their own kind, show a certain amount of parental care and consideration by not eating their babies! In some species the pups (baby sharks) are born in special "nursery grounds" in shallow water. The adult males rarely come to the area, and the females do not feed this time. Therefore the pups can get started in life, rather than being food for their cannibal parents!

MOUTH POUCH
The Asian bonytongue, *Scleropages*, is an attentive parent that broods its eggs, and then the young, in a large pouch-like part of its lower jaw. The fish is a member of a small but ancient and partially air-breathing fish group, the bonytongues, which also includes the acrobatic arawana (p. 37).

MOUTHFUL OF EGGS
The red-finned cichlids of Africa's Lake Malawi are fussy parents. The male clears a shallow scoop in a sandy or gravelly part of the lake bed. The female lays her eggs here; he fertilizes them; and then she delicately sucks them up and cares for them inside her mouth cavity for several weeks until they hatch.

Bright yellow bands of colour give this mouthbrooder its name

Young cichlid being "blown" out of mother's mouth

Cichlids remain near their mother in case danger threatens

Mouthbrooders

This term aptly describes a group of fishes that carry their eggs in their mouths. Even after hatching, the young fishes remain in the safety of their mother's "mouth nursery". Most mouthbrooders belong to the large cichlid family. The banded yellow mouthbrooder (right) is a cichlid, and lives in Africa's Lake Malawi.

OUT OF MOTHER'S MOUTH
The danger has passed. This banded yellow mouthbrooder "blows" her babies from her mouth, so that they can swim nearby and feed on minute floating plants and animals. It also allows this attentive mother to feed herself. When the fry are very young she holds them in her mouth for most of the time. As they grow, she gradually mouthbroods them less, until they only return to her mouth at night or when danger threatens. Inside the mouth, the young are well protected, and receive a constant stream of water carrying fresh supplies of oxygen for breathing.

CLINGING ON

Many young creatures cling on to their parents, including mammals. Monkeys (right) cling on to their mothers, but need to suck on a teat to get any nourishment.

PARENT NIBBLERS

The fry of the common brown discus fish, from South America, "eat" their parents! In this unique form of parental care, the male and female keep their eggs clean and well-fanned with their fins for four days after laying, until they hatch. After about a week the adults start to feed the young with special secretions made by their skin. The babies gather round in a cloud to nibble at the parent's secretions, which are produced to nourish the young and are completely different from the usual fishy mucous coating. Parent-nibbling continues for about four weeks until the young start to swim away freely.

STIRRING UP MUD

At breeding time, the male African lungfish makes a deep pit in the swampy mud, where his partner (or sometimes more than one) lays her eggs. The father then fiercely protects the eggs and hatchlings for up to two months. He snaps at predators and drives them away – and at 2 m (6 ft) long, he is a formidable sentry. He also swishes water through the nest by writhing body movements, to keep the young supplied with fresh water (and oxygen).

A fierce defender of his babies - the African lungfish

Living in harmony

The little pilot fish keeps sharks company as they swim along

Yellow anemone

MANY ANIMALS, including various fishes, can live in harmony together. Some fishes help others, and in the process help themselves. This type of relationship, which benefits all partners, is known as symbiosis. One amazing example involves tiny fishes known as cleaners, that swim trustingly right into the jaws of much bigger fishes. The cleaner's small mouth winkles out parasites and bits of stale food, which it swallows. So the cleaner gets a meal while the big fish gets a "wash and brush-up". Some fishes have evolved relationships with other kinds of animals. Clownfishes, damselfishes, and shepherd fishes shelter among poisonous sea anemone tentacles. This gives them a safe refuge, while the anemone may absorb pieces of food dropped by its guests as they feed; the guests may even act as "bait" to draw other fishes into the anemone's deadly grasp. Over 40 types of sea fishes live in or around sponges. Indeed, the possibilities for living in harmony seem endless . . .

Bubble anemone

LIFE IN A DEATH-TRAP
A large, jellyfish-like creature, the Portuguese man-o'-war is a terror to sea-life. Its stinging tentacles paralyze little fishes. But the little shepherd fish can swim unharmed amongst them. From the man-o'war it gains shelter, and food, and in return lures in fishes who are not resistant to the stings.

Clownfishes never stray far from the protection of the anemones.

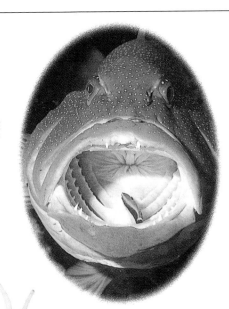

CLEANER AT WORK
A mutually beneficial partnership involves fishes called cleaners, such as certain small wrasses, and their customers. The wrasses wait at a regular cleaning station, often at the same time each day, and are approached by larger individuals that require service. The cleaner then picks fragments of food and parasites off the skin, fins, gills, and mouth - even right inside the throat. Here a tiny cleaner wrasse attends to a huge grouper in Australia's Barrier Reef.

Clown anemone

CLOWNING AROUND
On many tropical reefs, gaily coloured clownfishes dart among a forest of tentacles. Yet the tentacles belong to a sea anemone, and bear venomous stings which would paralyze other small fishes in seconds. For years, it was a mystery how the clownfishes could live in their deadly refuge, without succumbing and dying. Recent research has shown that the clownfish has an especially thick version of the mucous body covering possessed by many other fishes. Not only this, the mucus does not contain the usual "fishy" substances which stimulate the anemone to sting. The clownfish may also become smeared with some of the anemone's mucus, which gives it even greater protection. However, clownfishes cannot dash into the arms of any old anemone. The poison from a different type, such as the fire anemone below, is too strong, and it could be the end of a beautiful relationship.

Fire anemone

The clownfishes avoid this anemone - even they are not immune to its fiery sting

Snakes of the sea

MORAY'S FORAY
Morays grow to 3 m (10 ft) long and live in warm coastal waters around the world. Many are brightly coloured and are called "painted eels". Their formidable reputation makes them feared by divers.

Sᴸᴵᴹʏ ᴀɴᴅ ᴡᴏʀᴍʟɪᴋᴇ, eels are more like snakes than fishes, and glide through the water as snakes slither across land. They have been an important source of food since before Greek and Roman times - then, it was considered a symbol of wealth to have a pond of moray eels in captivity. They are elongated, tube-shaped fishes with apparently scaleless skin, no pelvic fins, and no spines in the remaining fins. There are about 600 species of true eels. These include freshwater eels, congers, morays, pike eels, and gulpers. Other fish groups have their own eel-shaped members, like the electric eel of South America, which is more closely related to the knifefishes and catfishes. Perhaps the most intriguing thing about eels is their breeding pattern, which remained a mystery to people until early this century (see right).

THE SERPENT'S TALE
For centuries, mariners have spun tales of great "sea serpents" terrifying their crews. Some sightings of these monsters may in fact be of large eels. More likely candidates include the oarfish, which grows to over 6 m (20 ft) long.

Pectoral fin

Gill opening

Yellow dorsal fin of ribbon eel

Pectoral fin

Skin is slimy and slippery

Front nostril

PELICAN EEL
The gulper eel is a deep-sea species that snaps at passing prey with its vast mouth.

Gulper eel

A TIGHT FIT
The gaily coloured ribbon eel is a type of moray. Like its cousins, it lurks in cracks and caves, waiting for prey to pass nearby. It then seizes the victim with a fast, snake-like strike of the head and a snap of the sharp-toothed jaws. The ribbon eel can coil itself backwards into crevices that seem far too small for its long body.

MYSTERIOUS MIGRATION

For centuries, the European eel's breeding habits were a mystery. Adult fishes lived in rivers and lakes, but each year, young eels (elvers) swam in from the sea in spring, and mature adults swam out to sea in the autumn. But eel eggs or larvae were never seen. Then in the 1920s, Danish zoologist Johannes Schmidt tracked the migrating eels to their breeding ground of the Sargasso Sea, in the West Atlantic. It is now thought that the adult eels spawn at great depth, and die. The eggs hatch into leaf-like larvae that live in the plankton. They drift towards Europe on the Gulf Stream current, arriving after two to three years. Now called leptocephali, they are transparent and do not resemble eels. Around Europe's coasts they change into glass eels or elvers, enter the rivers, and begin their growth to adulthood.

MIGRATION ROUTE OF EUROPEAN EEL

☐ Larvae metamorphose and enter rivers	☐ Larvae drift on Gulf Stream

European eels can glide through damp grass or slide through moist undergrowth to find a seaward river for migration

Dorsal fin

EEL BONES

A conger eel's skeleton reveals sharp, backward-pointing teeth from which escape is almost impossible. An eel's long, tubular body and astonishing capacity for writhing mean an immense number of vertebrae in the backbone – more than 100 in many cases. There are no pelvic or caudal (tail) fins, and many species lack pectoral fins too. The dorsal and anal fins stretch right to the end and join to form a continuous fringe around the back of the tail.

STUNNING EEL

The electric eel (right) dwells in oxygen-poor waters of the Amazon. Most of its body houses up to 6,000 electroplates - modified muscles arranged like tiny batteries. The eel can kill small fishes with 500-volt shocks, but uses much lower voltages to navigate through the murky water.

Sharp teeth

Rear nostril near eye

Great numbers of vertebrae in backbone for flexibility

Dorsal fin stretches right to the tail

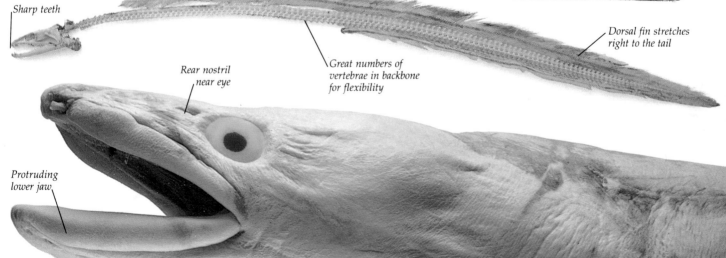

Protruding lower jaw

CONGER'S GAPE

The fearsome conger lunges at anything edible, from an octopus to the groping fingers of a skin diver (which may look quite similar). These eels spawn 4,000 m (13,000 ft) down in the mid-Atlantic.

Hidey holes

THE "LANDSCAPE" of the underwater world varies just as it does on land, from cool green gardens of seaweeds, to the dazzling corals of tropical reefs, to deserts of sand or gravel, to rocky and jagged cavern-ridden cliffs. Like the familiar caves, treetrunk holes, and soft soil we see on land, each of these watery habitats gives opportunities for hidey holes – which are useful for both predators and prey. Most of the hunted, like small wrasses, must feed out in the open; but at a second's notice they can dart out of harm's way, by digging them-selves into loose sand or mud, or diving into a narrow cleft in the rocks. Hunters like the moray eel (p. 48) and the shore goby are content to lurk in cracks and caves, watching for unsuspecting victims to swim past.

Eyespots are meant to intimidate predators by giving the illusion of a big "face"

Wrasse is searching for a loose patch of gravel to dive into

1 EMERGENCY!
The twinspot detects a threatening sound, or perhaps a worrying scent or the sight of a possible predator. At once it tilts its head down and, as it dives, searches out a bare patch of shelly gravel for refuge.

SAFE IN THE SAND
The twinspot wrasse, from tropical reefs, sports two large eyespots on its dorsal fin. If this huge "face" fails to frighten predators, the twinspot can dive into the coral sand or gravel and be out of sight within a few seconds. However, if the fish detects a "danger" and reacts, but the danger turns out to be harmless, the fish may gradually stop its reaction. This "fading away" of behaviour is known as habituation. Suppose a boulder became stuck in a gully and crashed to and fro in the waves. At first the wrasse might respond to the loud banging sounds by digging in every time. But gradually, if no danger appeared, it would come to ignore the noise. Which is just as well, since the boulder might bang on for months.

2 TESTING THE BED
As the fish reaches the seabed it swerves up to a horizontal position and thrusts its sensitive snout and chest into the gravel. If this should be only a shallow layer on top of solid rock and so no use for hiding, then the sooner the twinspot detects this, the better. Delay could mean death!

Wrasse's body is in a horizontal position and already throwing up gravel

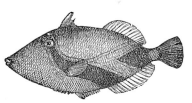

LOCKED FILE

The first spine of the filefish's dorsal fin has many tiny serrations, looking like a miniature version of a file (a ridged tool used for smoothing surfaces). However, its name came originally from the tiny spines on its scales, which give them a very rough texture, too. When in trouble, the filefish can swim into a crevice and lock its dorsal spine upright, as does its relative the triggerfish (p. 31). It is then wedged in and almost impossible to extract.

VANISHING GARDEN

Garden eels live in large groups in warm, shallow tropical waters (these are from the Caribbean). Each eel has its own burrow, regularly spaced from its neighbours. With its rear end "rooted" in the seabed it snaps at small floating plants and animals that pass by. It has very small fins but can wriggle forwards or backwards with surprising speed. Garden eels are named from their resemblance to a well-tended garden, waving gently in the "wind" of water currents. When disturbed, they rapidly slide backwards into their burrows and the entire "garden" disappears.

Loose gravel flung upwards by wrasse's activity

3 DIGGING IN
Throwing its body into S-shaped curves, digging down in a diagonal direction, the twinspot "swims" head first into the loose gravel and stones. Its fins and tail fling the gravel upwards out of the way.

Body is in an S-shaped curve, to burrow more efficiently

BOTTLED UP

This goby, a common shore fish, has taken refuge in the neck of a bottle. Fishes tend to treat man-made items with suspicion at first, but soon investigate their food value. As weeds and creatures slowly encrust the bottle, its artificial nature is obscured and it becomes just another useful "cave", for small fishes hiding from big ones, or for hunters waiting to ambush prey.

4 OUT OF SIGHT, OUT OF MIND
Within a few seconds, the fish is settled into the surface layer of stones, and the falling gravel rains back down to add to its covering. Here the twinspot stays until it senses that things are back to normal above. In fact many species of wrasse, especially around the Pacific coral islands, bury themselves in the gravel each night and go to "sleep" there. Others lie on their sides in caves and crevices. While the wrasses rest, the "night shift" of fishes take over and come out to feed and hunt on the reef.

Part of wrasse's body still visible in this photograph (but invisible to predators!)

Life on the move

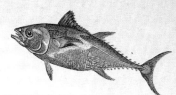

MANY KINDS OF FISHES SWIM TOGETHER in great groups called shoals and schools, or in looser collections called aggregates. Often, shoaling is connected with plankton feeding, as in the herring, the fishes following each other in their search for food-rich waters. Some species collect in great numbers in the breeding season. Gaining protection through "safety in numbers" is another reason why fishes swim in shoals, especially young fishes and smaller species. As a predator approaches a shoal, it is overcome by the bewildering numbers and activity, and is unable to pick out one individual prey. Small fishes in a dense shoal, moving in total unison, may gain protection by appearing as a single, much bigger creature. How do shoaling fishes achieve such harmony of movement? Eyesight plays a part; many shoaling species have distinct bars or spots, which members use as visual markers. The vibration-detecting lateral line (p. 7) also provides information about neighbours' movements.

WAITING WITH THE NETS
The great tuna shoals have dwindled in numbers today, mainly because of overfishing. Their yearly routine of entering the Mediterranean sea in early summer made them a predictable catch.

Darker back for countershading (p. 18)

SHOAL AS A WHOLE
Common dace of Europe (often called dares or darts) often swim in large shoals, especially when young. The fishes in the shoal dart and twist and turn in formation, moving together almost with one mind. In summer they swim just below the surface, often keeping to the shade under a tree, and rising to catch flies and other insects. The dace lives in fairly fast, clear, gravelly rivers. Yearlings are about 7 cm (3 in) long; adult dace reach 25 cm (10 in).

Lateral line runs low on body and can detect movements of other members of the shoal

Dashing habits of this fish give it the alternative name of dart

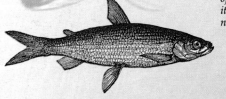

The Atlantic herring, which grows to 40 cm (16 in) long

TOO EASY TO CATCH
The decline in herring catches during the 1950s provides a clear example of overfishing. These fishes congregate in vast numbers and so are easy to net. In the days of sailboat fishing (above), catches were relatively constant. But modern boats, with shoal-locating radar and gigantic nets, are too efficient.

A LINK IN THE FOOD CHAIN
A huge group of Pacific herring move through the clear waters of Baja California, off the Mexican coast. Such density of numbers suits the fishing industry's seine nets and otter trawls. Herring are also a vital link in the natural food chains of the sea, being preyed on by many larger fishes and seabirds.

Yellowtail snappers of the western Atlantic hunt around reefs and rocks for smaller fishes and shellfish. This one is trying to feed on a dense shoal of small herring-like fishes. The shoal darts to and fro with confusing rapidity. The snapper may become so confused that, despite the number of tasty titbits before its eyes, it ends up being unable to single out one to snap at.

Shoals mill around in seeming confusion when they are changing direction

Eyes can look up and down

White underside

Silvery side

Poisonous fishes

MORE THAN 50 KINDS of poisonous fishes swim in the world's waters. Every year, people become severely ill or even die from the poison (also called venom or toxin) of stingrays, weevers, stonefishes, lionfishes, and other species. But these fishes did not evolve their venom in order to threaten humans. They use it mainly as a defence, to harm larger predators such as big flatfishes and rays when they attack. Unpleasant effects of fish poisoning on humans include numbness, paralysis, difficulty in breathing. uncontrolled bleeding, and blood poisoning.

So-called because of its skyward-looking eyes, the stargazer's poison spines are above the pectoral fins

Thin, whippy tail

Delicate patterned tail

Three venomous anal spines

Sting is a "dagger" of bone set into tail

Dinner or death?

Some fishes have flesh that, when eaten, is poisonous to humans. Certain types of pufferfishes are especially toxic. But the poison, tetrodotoxin, is limited to specific body parts of the fish. The flesh (muscle) itself is said to be relatively safe and quite tasty. In Japan pufferfish (also called glovefish) is served in restaurants as the delicacy "fugu", where specially trained chefs prepare and cook the catch. Even so, despite various safeguards, severe illness and even death still occur when fugu has been prepared incorrectly.

Dead pufferfish awaiting preparation

THE RAY'S STING
The venom of a stingray's sting is made in shiny white tissue running along the two grooves on the spine's underside. In the European species the spine is about 12 cm (5 in) long. In larger tropical species it may reach up to 40 cm (16 in).

STING IN THE TAIL
More than 100 species of stingrays lurk in coastal shallows around the world. Some grow to great size, with a "wingspan" of more than 3 m (10 ft) and weighing well over 300 kg (661 lb). They tend to hide in the bottom sand and sediment, or glide along slowly as they search for shellfish and fishes to crack and crush with their rows of blunt teeth. When in trouble, these rays bring the sting into play. The sting is a spine-shaped, iron-hard "dagger" of bone set into the tail near its base. Some stingrays have two or even three stings. The thin, whippy tail is of little use for swimming, but it is excellent as a stinging tool. Under threat, the ray lashes its tail to and fro or even arches it over the head, slashing with its sting and stabbing it into the enemy. Besides the venom, the sting's sharp, serrated edges can inflict jagged cuts. The poison acts quickly on humans, bringing on pain and swelling, and affecting the nervous system to cause problems with breathing and heartbeat. In severe cases, death follows.

A pufferfish in pieces and ready for preparation. A keen eye is needed to identify the poisonous organs

Eating fugu: compliments to the chef - if still alive afterwards!

Thirteen venomous dorsal spines

Eye

DEADLY BEAUTY

Lionfish, scorpionfish, zebrafish, dragonfish, turkeyfish, firefish - call it what you will, this colourful and ornate creature is one of the most poisonous in the sea. The spiny rays in its decorative, lacy fins house glands which make a powerful venom that can disable predators, and has been reported as fatal to interfering humans. The lionfish grows up to 40 cm (16 in) long and graces shallow waters around reefs and rocks, in warm regions from the Red Sea across the Indian Ocean to Australia and the Pacific. Its graceful fins and splendid striped coloration advertize the fact that this fish is not to be tampered with. For much of the time it swims lazily along, fins waving slowly, ignoring predators in the knowledge that its bright red-brown stripy body signal one of nature's warning patterns. However, the lethargic manner is deceptive. If the lionfish spots a small fish or shellfish that looks a likely prey, it can dart forward and strike with lightning speed.

STONY FACED

Like the lionfish, the stonefish is a member of the scorpionfish family. But unlike its colourful cousin, it has a warty, blotched body that blends perfectly into the stony seabed. This fish even allows weeds and anemones to grow on its skin, to aid camouflage. In defence, the fish raises the spines along its back. These can inject the most potent of all fish venoms, even through the soles of beach shoes. A sting can maim, or even kill.

Two venomous pectoral spines

Lionfish spine

Venom gland

Sheath

IN THE GROOVE
Each lionfish spine bears a venom gland lying in a long central groove. The entire spine is also sheathed in glandular tissue.

Spiny fin ray

Base of ray

Eye of stingray

Large pectoral fin

Serrated edge

Sting contains venom made in shiny white tissue

BE WARY OF THE WEEVER

The lesser weever (viperfish) lies partly buried in sand, waiting for its food of small shellfish, crabs, and fish. If molested, (or stepped upon unwittingly) defensive venom flows from glands at the bases of the erected, grooved spines on the gill covers and first dorsal fin.

All about rays

STRANGE AND GRACEFUL COUSINS OF SHARKS, the rays belong to a group comprising about 300 species, including skates and sawfishes. Because of their shape, they are often confused with flatfishes – but there are several basic differences. Rays, like sharks, have skeletons made of cartilage – they lack the true bony skeleton of the flatfishes. And whereas flatfishes lie on their sides, rays are flattened from top to bottom and lie in the normal way, on their bellies. This could pose problems in breathing, since gills on the underside could become clogged by seabed mud. But rays have evolved a circular opening just behind each eye, the spiracle, which admits cleaner water into the gill chambers. Most rays stay on or near the seabed and feed by grinding up fishes, shellfish, worms and other bottom-dwellers with their flattened teeth.

A member of the ray group, the sawfish uses its distinctive saw-like snout in defence

Large, moveable eye (rays have good eyesight)

Snout is sensitive to touch as the ray noses in seabed mud

Spiracle - entrance for water to the gills as the ray lies on the bottom

Fin rays (struts) completely covered by flesh and skin, unlike bony fishes

Main row of thorns or bucklers along backbone

Back is colour camouflaged to conceal ray over sand, gravel, rocks, pebbles, and mud

Back view of female thornback ray

THORNBACK'S BACK
The thornback ray, also called the roker, is closely related and similar in appearance to the larger common skate. Thornbacks reach about 1 m (3 ft), while skates grow to nearer 2 m (6 ft). This common species of ray is well camouflaged when lying on pebbly mud or sand. It rarely strays to waters deeper than 50 m (164 ft), and during the summer breeding season adults stay in shallower water. Young thornbacks feed on small fishes and shrimps. As they mature, they also begin to eat larger shrimps, crabs, and other shellfish, as well as flatfishes, sprats, and sand eels.

Dorsal fin

Bucklers along back

Thornback ray in resting pose

RAY AT REST
The aptly named thornback lies in its resting pose, showing off the main row of defensive rosebush-like thorns, called bucklers. These are projections of the backbone, or spine, along its back and tail. There are also spines on the sides of the tail, and two small dorsal fins towards its end. It holds its body slightly arched, to allow a free flow of water through the gill clefts on the underside.

NO BONES ABOUT RAYS
Being a cartilaginous fish, the thornback's skeleton consists of cartilage, not bone. The strut-like pectoral fin rays are expanded like a fan to form the flexible framework for the "wings" (compare with the fossil ray on page 11).

Nostril, opening to olfactory (smell) organ and guarded by a flap (rays hunt largely by scent)

Horny mouth adapted for grasping shellfish and other bottom-living creatures

reatly expanded pectoral ns are joined to head to ve typical diamond-haped ray outline

Five gill clefts, one for each gill arch inside the gill chamber

A GIANT AMONG RAYS

The Atlantic manta or "devil-fish" is the largest living ray, weighing in at well over 2 tons and with a wing-span exceeding 6 m (20 ft). It has a long, thin tail, and lobed "scoops" (adapted from the front parts of the pectoral fins) on the front of the head to channel food into the great mouth. Despite their overwhelming size, mantas have small teeth and are gentle filter-feeders, cruising the upper waters of warm oceans and consuming plankton, small fishes, and shellfish. They can also leap up to 1.5m (5 ft) from the water. Their name comes from the Spanish for "blanket" and refers to the wide, mantle-like pectoral fins.

Electric organs (electricity-producing muscle blocks)

Nerves controlling electric organs

Electric ray sectioned to show electric organs

Spines on underside

Ray swims by up-and-down undulating motion of its pectoral fins, "flying" through the water

Small pelvic fins

Underside of female thornback ray

WHAT A FACE!

Like the flatfishes, the ray does not need to have a coloured underside, since it is usually on the seabed and so rarely seen. The nostrils and mouth form a curiously cheerful human-looking "face", and the cartilaginous fin struts are visible through the pale skin.

Atlantic torpedo or electric ray

SHOCKING RAY

Like several other fish groups, rays have their high-powered electricity-generating members. There are about 35 species of electric rays. One is the Atlantic torpedo or electric ray. It grows to more than 1.5 m (5 ft) in length. Like most rays, it lies lazily on the seabed for much of the time, but occasionally stirs itself to feed. The torpedo preys on small shellfish and fishes. As the ray swoops it wraps its pectoral fins around the victim and delivers shocks of over 200 volts from specialized muscle blocks on either side of its head.

The great warriors of the sea

Face to face with a fearsome fish foe: the dangerous end of a blue shark showing its mouthful of teeth

Thresher has a short, blunt snout

Large eyes for hunting by vision (threshers have better eyesight than most sharks)

Nostrils for hunting by scent

A TRIANGULAR FIN breaking the surface of an otherwise calm sea is something that strikes dread into the hearts of swimmers. Beneath the fin is the creature we love to hate, a fish whose predatory menace and mastery of the sea has made it infamous - the shark. Many sharks are powerful and efficient killing machines. They detect a likely prey with their finely tuned senses (including eyesight, smell, and electricity-detecting organs around the nose), then charge at sudden speed, and bite with bone-crunching power. Yet not all sharks are ferocious, sleek, and streamlined. The wobbegongs or carpet sharks of the Eastern Pacific and Australia are slow movers, which rarely attack people unless severely provoked, and feed on bottom-dwelling shellfish. Their rounded, flattish bodies are mottled with yellows, oranges, and browns, to help camouflage them as they lie among the rocks and weeds of the seabed.

Small triangular teeth for grabbing prey

A shark's gill slits are separate and not covered by an operculum

THE PRIMITIVE HUNTER

Sharks are often called "primitive" creatures. This means that they appeared quite early in the evolution of the fish group, and they have survived largely unchanged, at least on the outside, for millions of years. However, in this sense, "primitive" does not imply that sharks are now out of date. Theirs was a highly successful design first time around, and only slight changes have occured since. An early type of shark was the 2 m (6 ft) long *Cladoselache*, which terrorized the seas 350 million years ago. The frilled shark, a "living leftover", seems to have become "stuck" at an early stage of shark evolution. It looks like species of *Cladoselache's* time more than modern sharks.

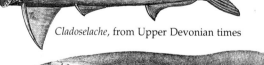

Cladoselache, from Upper Devonian times

Frilled shark, a rare living deep-water species

THRASHING THRESHER

The thresher's remarkable tail (which is so long that it extends to page 61) accounts for this shark's various common names: fox shark, whiptail, thrasher, swiveltail, and swingle tail. The tail is used as a "thrash". The shark circles a shoal of smaller fishes, such as mackerel, pilchard, or herring, and sweeps them into a tight group by swishing up the water with whips of its tail. It then charges through the shoal open-mouthed, and snaps up dazed victims. Some people claim that the thresher can stun a fish with one blow of its tail, and flick it into its mouth with the next. One specimen caught had a stomach bulging with 25 mackerel, so the thresher is certainly a keen feeder. This species lives in warmer coastal waters in the Atlantic and eastern Pacific, although in summer it strays to cooler seas off northern Europe and New England, U.S.A. The thresher grows to 6 m (20 ft) long but only attains 450 kg (992 lb) in weight, since its tapering tail makes up half the overall length.

INSIDE STORY

Sharks are cartilaginous fishes, which means that they have skeletons made not of bone, but of cartilage. However the cartilage is not soft and rubbery, but extremely hard - as shown by the power of a shark's bite (p. 61). This catshark skeleton shows how the rear end of the spine turns up into the upper lobe of the heterocercal tail (p. 30). The claspers on the pelvic fins show that this is a male: female sharks do not have claspers.

Skin bears marks and scars of previous hunting encounters

Typical shark's triangular dorsal fin

Dark grey upper part of body

HEAD LIKE A HAMMER

Various theories try to explain the hammerhead's amazing shape. The great distance between the eyes and nostrils may allow the shark to detect its prey's direction more accurately. Or the flat head may work like a wing as the shark swims, to give extra lift to the front of the body. Whatever the reason, hammerheads are experts at catching the stingrays on which they feed.

Small, bump-like second dorsal fin

FILM STAR

Jaws was a great white shark or maneater (p. 61). These sharks grow to 9 m (30 ft) - big, but not the giant suggested by the publicity.

White underside to body (see countershading, p. 18)

Large scythe-shaped pectoral fin

Small pelvic fins

SHARK'S BIRTHDAY

Some shark mothers lay eggs (oviparity, p. 42). Others keep the eggs inside, while the young develop and are nourished by their yolk sacs (ovo-viviparity). Some young sharks retain the yolk sac for a while after birth. Yet others nourish their young directly from their own blood supply, and give birth to fully-formed young (viviparity).

Continued on next page

The warrior's weapons

The word "shark" seems to be unavoidably linked with "teeth". They are certainly well supplied with them, in fact sharks never stop growing new teeth. In most species the teeth are triangular or pointed, with sharp tips and serrated edges - a sure sign of a hunter. In a typical shark attack, if the prey is too big to eat in one gulp, the shark will clamp its teeth on the victim's body and shake its head from side-to-side, "sawing" off a mouth-sized lump.

LION-EATING TIGER
The wide-open mouth of a tiger shark displays rows of razor-sharp teeth in the upper and lower jaws. This species grows to 6 m (20 ft) in length and weighs as much as 15-20 adult humans. As the shark attacks, its jaws swing forward and outwards, its snout turns up and out of the way, and its eyes roll inwards in their sockets: all this helps the creature to get a clean snap at the prey. Tiger sharks eat whatever they can, from sea lions to squid, turtles, and other sharks.

Tiger on the prowl: in warm seas worldwide, the tiger shark hunts in as little as 1 m (3 ft) of water

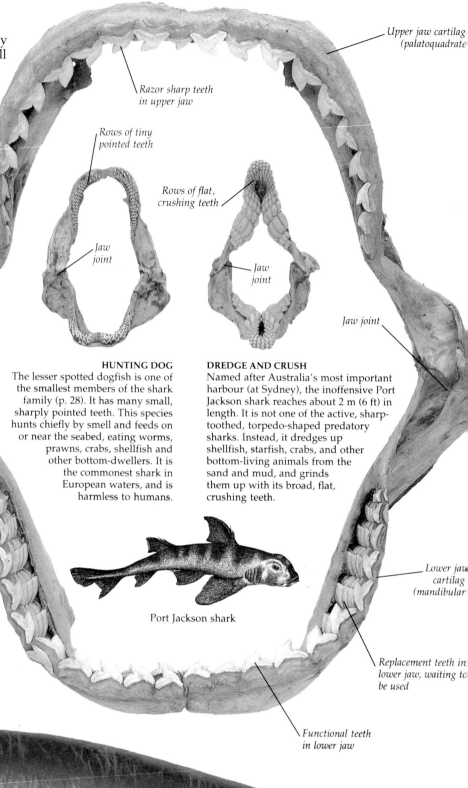

Razor sharp teeth in upper jaw

Rows of tiny pointed teeth

Rows of flat, crushing teeth

Jaw joint

Jaw joint

Upper jaw cartilage (palatoquadrate)

Jaw joint

Lower jaw cartilage (mandibular)

Replacement teeth in lower jaw, waiting to be used

Functional teeth in lower jaw

HUNTING DOG
The lesser spotted dogfish is one of the smallest members of the shark family (p. 28). It has many small, sharply pointed teeth. This species hunts chiefly by smell and feeds on or near the seabed, eating worms, prawns, crabs, shellfish and other bottom-dwellers. It is the commonest shark in European waters, and is harmless to humans.

DREDGE AND CRUSH
Named after Australia's most important harbour (at Sydney), the inoffensive Port Jackson shark reaches about 2 m (6 ft) in length. It is not one of the active, sharp-toothed, torpedo-shaped predatory sharks. Instead, it dredges up shellfish, starfish, crabs, and other bottom-living animals from the sand and mud, and grinds them up with its broad, flat, crushing teeth.

Port Jackson shark

Small lower lobe of thresher's tail

BIGGEST HAS THE SMALLEST

The world's biggest shark (and biggest of all fishes, p. 6) has some of the smallest teeth. Whale sharks have rows of "teeth" (modified denticles) in the mouth, along their gills, and in the throat and gullet. These act as a sieve to filter small floating creatures from the water, as the shark cruises along slowly at about human walking speed.

Very long upper lobe of thresher's tail

Rows of whale shark teeth

Small teeth made from modified denticles (placoid scales, p. 14)

Basking shark

BASKER'S TEETH
A basking shark (the second-largest of all fishes) has many small teeth, but these are probably evolutionary leftovers. This great creature, 9 m (30 ft) long, feeds by sieving the water with its gill rakers (p. 9).

Lower jaw cartilage from basking shark

THRESHER'S THRASH
The thresher's tail is extremely muscular, tough, and strong, like a thick leather strap, and can be flexed (bent) at will. A trapped thresher can do immense damage to the nets and other captive fishes, as its tail (caudal fin) whips to and fro.

Fossil shark tooth is shown at less than actual size

TOOTHY JAILERS
Some prisons and captive colonies, such as Devil's Island off French Guyana, were located on islands in shark-infested waters. The sharks made short work of convicts attempting to escape.

FOSSIL HUNTER
Prehistoric shark skeletons, being made of cartilage, are preserved less often as fossils compared to bony skeletons. However the shark's extremely hard teeth have fossilized well. This great white shark fossil tooth is in fact as big as a human hand. This indicates that predatory white sharks such as *Procarcharodon* (of 20 million years ago) grew to almost 13 m (43 ft) in length!

WHITE DEATH
The great white is the most feared of all shark species. Experiments with a "bite-meter" show that a big shark can exert a force of 60 kg (132 lb) through just one tooth! The total biting pressure is many tonnes. Above is the skeleton of the jaws, which are slung loosely beneath the snout and the rest of the skull.

A living legend: the fearsome great white shark looms out of the water

NEW TEETH
A shark continuously grows new teeth at the backs of its jaws. These gradually move forward, conveyor-belt fashion, until they reach the front of the mouth, where they swing outwards ready for use. As the working teeth wear away or break off, new ones from behind take their place. These are the distinctive spear-like teeth of a mako (blue pointer), an extremely fast and ferocious species.

Exposed teeth ready for use

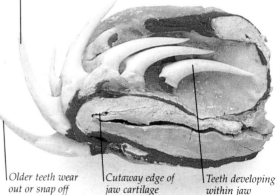

Older teeth wear out or snap off

Cutaway edge of jaw cartilage

Teeth developing within jaw

Studying fishes

I**N LABORATORIES** and scientific stations around the world, from the frozen Arctic to the steaming tropics, fishes are being studied by scientists. A lot of these are ichthyologists, or fish specialists (*ichthys* is the Greek for fish). It is more than simple curiosity. Many of the world's peoples rely on fishes for food, especially for the protein part of their diet. Fish populations are constantly monitored, to assess whether overfished species are regaining their numbers, and to identify new stocks which could find their way into trawlers' nets. Most fishes are sensitive to small quantities of strange chemicals in the water, and their sickness or disappearance from rivers, lakes, and seas shows that pollution has occurred. Healthy waters mean healthy fishes: they have twice as much of the Earth to swim in than we have to walk on, and they ultimately reflect the health of our planet.

DARWIN'S FISHES
During his voyage around the world in HMS Beagle, in the 1830s, the eminent naturalist Charles Darwin collected and studied many fish species. A sea-bass from Chile is shown ready for study at his desk (left). He described a porcupine fish that had been swallowed by a shark but then apparently eaten its way out through the shark's side: "Who would ever have imagined that a little soft fish could have destroyed the great and savage shark?"

Flexible spotlight for studying specimens under the microscope

Angled seeker or probe for parting blocks of tissue and various organs

Needle or ligament scalpel for cutting nerves

Fine scalpel for cutting muscles and vessels

SEE-THROUGH STAINING
Fish bodies are preserved and prepared using various chemicals, depending on what is to be studied. In the alizarin technique, the creature's flesh and soft organs are turned to a transparent jelly, and the harder parts such as bones and fin rays are stained deep pink by the alizarin dye (obtained originally from the madder plant of India). The complete skeleton can then be studied under the microscope, revealing the shapes and proportions of the various bones.

TOOLS FOR THE JOB
Various specialized instruments are needed to examine the internal structure of a fish's body. The bones, muscles, and ligaments are tough and strong, and it requires great skill and care to expose the organs without damaging them.

Bone chisel for cutting through tough outer scutes and thick bone

Scalpel for cutting through outer skin and scales

Fine forceps or tweezers for lifting out various vessels and small organs for study

Syringe and hypodermic needle for injecting preservatives into fish

FISH GALLERY
Reference books and catalogues help to identify a new or unfamiliar specimen. Photographs cannot lie, but often a good painting is better at conveying the essential features of a species

X-RAY FISH
The bones and cartilages of fishes, like those of humans, show up as white on an X-ray screen (below). Such images can be used to study the bone structure of living fishes, showing how they develop and age, and also to investigate fish diseases.

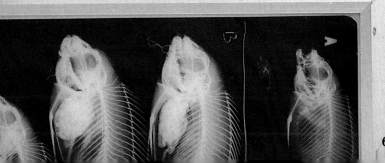

IN GOOD SPIRITS

Fish specimens are first "fixed" in formalin to stop the tissues decaying. They [ar]e then stored permanently [in] alcohol. The colours tend to fade, but every detail of the internal structure is preserved.

Tight-fitting lid to prevent evaporation of spirit

Suitably shaped glass spirit jar

MORE THAN WORDS CAN SAY

As the ichthyologist works on a fish, he or she makes notes on and draws sketches of significant points. A diagram of how the head bones fit together, drawn from an actual specimen, is usually clearer than a photograph and easier to understand than a written description.

Ichthyologist's notes and sketches made during a dissection

[U]NDER THE MICROSCOPE

[Va]rious types of microscopes [are] used to look at the fish in [gr]eater and greater detail. A [bi]nocular or dissecting [mi]croscope (above) reveals [par]ts that are slightly too [sm]all for the naked eye, at a [ma]gnification of about 10-50 [tim]es. The scanning electron [mi]croscope or SEM (right) [sh]ows surface details at over [10],000 times life-sized.

Two eyepieces of binocular microscope give 3D "depth" to the view, unlike a single-eyepiece microscope

Modern technology: a scientist working on a scanning electron microscope (SEM)

MEASURING FISHES

The dial calipers are one of several accurate instruments for measuring the size of fish features, from the height of the tail to the diameter of an eye or a tiny scale. Such information is recorded in tables and charts (right).

Dial calipers

RAW DATA

Sets of basic measurements of fishes and other information are analyzed, often by computer, and compiled into a "database summary" for that particular fish or group of fishes. This data can be used to tell species apart, or the number of fishes there are in a species. The information may then be published in scientific journals and communicated to other experts.

Raw data for computers

Index

Acknowledgments

Dorling Kindersley would like to thank:
Geoff Potts, Fred Frettsome, and Vicky Irlam at the Marine Biological Association, Plymouth; Rick Elliot and the staff at Waterlife Research Industries Ltd; Neil Fletcher; Harold Taylor; Simon Newnes & Partners, Billingsgate, London; Richard Davies of OSF for photography on pp. 28–29, 32–33; Bari Howell at MAFF, Conwy for supplying eggs and hatchlings on pp. 24–25; Barney Kindersley; Lester Cheeseman and Jane Coney for additional design work; Jane Parker for the index.

Picture credits

t=top b=bottom m=middle l=left r=right

Ardea: 37mr, 58tl
Biofotos/Heather Angel: 32tl
Anthony Blake/Roux Bros: 42tl
Bruce Coleman Ltd/Kim Taylor: 43tl
Philip Dowell: 18tl, 18ml, 18br
Mary Evans Picture Library: 6tl, 14ml, 17tr, 20tl, 30ml, 30tr, 61bl
Robert Harding Picture Library: 29br, 55tl
Dave King: 27mr
Kobal Collection: 59bl
Frank Lane Picture Agency/Stevie McCutcheon: 28tr
David Morbey/Natural History Museum: 63m
A. Van den Nieuwenhuizen: 28b
Planet Earth Pictures: 44tr, 44ml, 53tl, 60bl; James King: 52bl; John & **Gillian Lythgoe:** 49tr;

Jane McKinnon: 23tm; Paulo Oliveira: 45tl; Peter Scoones: 11br, 51tr; Bill Wood: 47t
Gary Summons/Natural History Museum: 62t
Survival Anglia/Alan Root: 33tr
Frank Spooner Pictures: 54m, 54bm, 54bl
Zefa/J. Schupe: 7tr

Illustrations by: John Woodcock

Picture research by: Kathy Lockley